The Golfer's Cookbook

Compiled by Rose Elder

*I hope my book will demand equal space
on your cookbook shelves*

— Rose Elder

DEDICATION

To my brothers and sisters; Gene, Millie, Sonny, Skippy, Jackie, Bobby, Michael and Michele, (with the exception of Mike and Michele) who had to eat my cooking whether they liked it or not. (When we were growing up all the girls had to alternate and cook the meals when our mother and grandmother were at work). They used to frown up their faces and say "gosh, this is awful, *what is it?"* Now they are kind . . . they smile and say; "it's lovely, what is it?".

To my loveable and faithful cousin, Raymond . . . who means so much to us all, also my Uncle Lenwood.

To my beautiful and precious grandmother, Dora Head, she is my tower of strength, she made sure with the help of my mother that all her grandchildren were taught to love and respect one another, to honor and obey your parents. She gave her life to us and she still looks after us all today.

To "Zsa Zsa" & "Birdie" my two little girls . . . they run the house.

To my loving husband Lee, who allowed me the time, gave his support and encouragement to allow me to complete this project. He is my number one fan, he not only raves about every meal I prepare for him . . . he makes sure the wine is always just right.

To my Dad who passed away August 1954 and my mother who passed away August 1973

"God gave us a memory, that we might have roses in December. You both are my roses"

Contents

ACKNOWLEDGMENTS

A special thanks to Joe Rauscher for his kind personal involvement and interest in the Lee Elder Scholarship Fund.

My thanks to the Community Relations Office of the Potomac Electric Power Company in Washington, D.C. where some of the recipes were tested in its test kitchens. Also to the Home Economics Department of the District of Columbia Public Schools and the students and teachers who prepared the food during these sessions.

To Patricia Spaulding, Editor Alumni News, Howard University who undertook the painstaking chore of editing. (A personal contribution to the Foundation)

And I am grateful to my dear friend Jean Payne who diligently prepared the groundwork, requesting and collecting these many recipes, without whose help the project would still be "on the ground."

PHOTOGRAPHY: Yoichi R. Okamoto
The White House Official Photographers

SKETCHES: Vernel Duvall

CREDITS:
- "Other Wild Rice Recipes" courtesy of Munsingwear booklet, *Mah-No-Min, The Indian Word for Wild Rice.* (Minneapolis, Minn.)
- From *Five Star Favorites* by Desert Charities, Inc., 1974:
  Granny's Homemade Ice Cream
  Maxwell's Meat Loaf
  Pork Chops with Barbecue Sauce
  Ranger Cookies
  Stuffed Pork Chops
  Jack's Favorite Prune Cake with Sauce
  Arnie's Favorite Beef Stew
  Pineapple Pavlova
  Dolores Hope, Antipasto Salad
- "Baking Basics," from *Family Circle Great Ideas,* January 1977.

Rose Elder Recipe Testing Project

The author acknowledges the assistance provided by the following home economics teachers and students who participated in a District of Columbia Public Schools Project—the Rose Elder Recipe Testing Project—at PEPCO and at school sites which are listed below.

BALLOU SENIOR HIGH SCHOOL—*Mrs. Mary Brooks, Teacher and Mrs. Joyce Law, Teacher*

Dena Dickerson, Joseph Langeley, Davine Kimble, Cornelius Jackson, Yolanda Lucas, Steve Sherrod, Keith Williams, Lamont Finney, Tyrone Nickols, Joyce Harley.

BURDICK CAREER CENTER—*Mrs. Elsie Reed, Teacher*

Lolita Butler, Camelia Gillard, Dorothy Gilliard, Ruby Jenkins, Stephanie Williams.

CARDOZO SENIOR HIGH SCHOOL—*Mrs. Margie W. Wade, Teacher and Miss Diane Hopkins, Student Teacher, Federal City College*

Sheila Crowe, Adriene Norman, Gloria Jackson, Theresa Quattlebaum, Renee Tyler, Melvenia Washington.

CALVIN COOLIDGE SENIOR HIGH SCHOOL—*Mrs. Josie M. Cole, Teacher and Mrs. Ethelene Mason, Assistant Teacher*

David Calhoun, Verna Howell, Michele Kemp, Roland Hercules, Ellsworth Hercules, Pamela Owens, Karen Priestly, Crystal Samuels, Valerie Smith.

EASTERN SENIOR HIGH SCHOOL—*Mrs. Dorothy Lee, Teacher*

Maria Banks, Valerie Adams, Darryl Clemons, Cohen Cosby, Stanyz Loving, TaWanna C. Jones, Willie Gross.

MACFARLAND JUNIOR HIGH SCHOOL—*Mrs. Anna L. Shelton, Teacher*

Veronica Hicks, Angela Logan, Angela Dade, Deidra McCurdy, Adrienne Smoot, Valerie Butler, LaWanda Musgrove, Sheila Harrison, Stephanie Bridges.

ROOSEVELT SENIOR HIGH SCHOOL—*Mrs. Sallie Simpson, Teacher*

Margaret Carter, Betty Fitzgerald, Karen Bumper, Karen Irving, Gwendolyn Sidert, Gwendolyn Byrd, Julia Johnson, Renee Upshur.

SPINGARN SENIOR HIGH SCHOOL—*Mrs. Irene Blum, Teacher*

Annette Anthony, Linda Briscoe, Pamela Morton, John Mullen, Maurice Parker, Jessifer Quinerly, Michael Shield, Walter Shorter, Andrea Tyler, Barbara West.

H. D. WOODSON SENIOR HIGH SCHOOL—*Mrs. Emma King, Teacher*

Sharon Booth, Derother Bowman, Gail Cook, Kenneth Gerald, Valaria Henderson, Miriam Hemphill, Weslley James, Jackie Lloyd, Wayne Mack, Reggie Pegram, Pamela Terry, Bernard Williams, Maria Banks

DUNBAR SENIOR HIGH SCHOOL—*Mrs. Willie B. Friday, Teacher and Mrs. Evelyn Primas, Student Teacher*

Joann Anderson, Deborah Armstrong, Gwendolyn Brown, Karen Gray, Portia Baker, Willie Parson, Michael Green, Debbie Wilson, Patricia Jackson, Bernadette Smith.

Special acknowledgment goes to Mrs. Barbara A. Ramos, Supervising Director of Home Economics Education, and Mrs. Annie M. McElrath, Acting Assistant Supervising Director of Home Economics Education.

Introduction

I write this introduction not for profit, nor even friendship. Rather it is inspired by a passion . . . for Rose Elder's cooking.

The world seems to insist on regarding her husband as the family celebrity which, of course, is the sheerest sort of nonsense. He merely slashes at a small white ball with a stick. Granted, with what I understand to be a certain skill. His primary role in life, however, is as receptable for the thousand delights which spring to existence in and on the Elder family stove, to the culinary art what Merlin's wand was to magic.

While Rose Elder's talents in the kitchen are belied by a trim figure, only the briefest glance at her husband is necessary to assure the reader that this book has much more to recommend it than printed information. While Lee Elder is not rotund, neither is he usually described as svelte. In short, his girth is, well, ample. And testimony to his wife's skills and the credibility of the recipes herein contained.

Elder, himself, will not comment beyond the admission that "I do like to eat and Rose is a great cook."

I could not agree more, having broken bread with the Elders many times. Often it is their misfortune to discover me at their front door, belly empty and nose quivering mightily in the general direction of the kitchen. Which is where I first met Rose . . . over coffee and homemade Danish. Lee and I were introduced over a hot dog and in short order, he took me to a Chinese restaurant where the *maitre'd* almost pulled a hamstring muscle while whisking us to the finest table in the house. "I eat here once in a while," Lee explained. Busboys waved at him from the kitchen.

Good things to eat even seem to follow the Elders around, the master of the house seeming to serve as some sort of Pied Piper for cooks obviously recognizing in him the ideal in consumptive devices.

There are circles in which Lee Elder is regarded as the professional golf tour's answer to the Galloping Gourmet. "Don't sit on Elder's right," being an enduring a pro golf term as "you're away."

In Augusta two years ago, as Lee was playing the Masters as the first black golfer ever to grace that sanctified event, the real intrigue was taking place in the kitchen of the house the Elders had rented for their stay.

The name of the woman cooking for the Elders that week escapes me; the memory of her considerable talents is forever imbedded in my taste buds. No one should pass from this mortal soil without having sampled this lady's Sweet Potato Cobbler. "A man playing golf for a living needs his strength," Lee explained.

Suffice it to conclude that the deadly sin of gluttony, if not accomplished in the Elder home, is at least approached. Rose was trained in the art by her mother and grandmother, the skills of two generations having accrued to a third. Cookbooks were used but not abused, cooking not a science but an art which wants, as Rose puts it, "just some of this and some of that."

Some of this and that may be found in the recipes provided by these courageous women who depend upon the treacherous course of a struck ball for the family well-being.

So search out this book for the good things to eat with the assurance that if Gerald Ford and Sammy Davis Jr. and Lee Elder like them, your favorite trencherman probably will, too.

Eat . . . enjoy.

—Phil Musick
Pittsburgh Post Gazette

Foreword

There are always lots of recipes, however, it is really the individual that adds personal feelings to make a dish really theirs. Herein are some of my friends' wisdom and special skills of their home cooks and friends who have shared their meals as well as their homes and kitchens and even their favorite markets around the country to give me these mostly practical to simple and exotic and delicious personal recipes. Most of the cooking is very basic and down to earth, simple to prepare and serve. Although the days of my grandmother's cooking is a thing of the past, a good cook is still a practical cook.

My sincere appreciation to all the golfers' wives who submitted their families' favorite recipes and to those who did not, I hope you will enjoy your friend's selections.

This project was initiated in 1975 and all names were taken from the current player's roster at that time; therefore, some of your favorite players' names might not appear on our pages.

Approximate Weights of Some Commodities in Avoirdupois Ounces Per Cup

Beans (dry) 6½
Butter, margarine, cooking oils 8
Citrus Fruit juice (fresh) 8½
Cornflakes 1
Corn meal 5
Eggs (whole) 8½
Flour (wheat, all-purpose, sifted) 4
Flour (cake, sifted) 3½
Milk (whole, fluid) 8½
Milk (dry) 4½

Nutmeats (pecan) 4
Oatmeal 3
Pancake mix 5
Prunes (dried) 5½
Raisins (seedless) 5
Rice 7
Shortening (vegetable) 7
Sugar (brown, moist, firmly packed) . 7½
Sugar (granulated) 7
Water 8⅓

Abbreviations Used in This Book

tsp.—teaspoon or teaspoons
tbs.—tablespoon or tablespoons
pkg.—package
pkgs.—packages
pt.—pint
pts.—pints
qt.—quart
qts.—quarts
oz.—ounce or ounces
lb.—pound
lbs.—pounds

BAKING BASICS*

DICTIONARY OF BAKING TERMS

- **Bake:** To cook with dry heat, usually in an oven.
- **Batter:** A combination of flour, liquid and other ingredients of dropping or pouring consistency.
- **Beat:** The term formerly referred to as "cream," meaning to stir vigorously with a spoon, egg beater, wire whip or electric mixer, as in combining sugar and butter.
- **Blend:** To thoroughly combine two or more ingredients until very smooth.
- **Boil:** To heat until bubbles rise continuously and break on surface of liquid (212° at sea level); a rolling boil has rapidly forming bubbles.
- **Brown:** To cook until food changes color, as with butter or nuts.
- **Caramelize:** To heat sugar slowly in a heavy pan until it turns brown in color and caramel in flavor.
- **Chop:** To cut food into pieces with a knife, mechanical chopper, or other sharp tool, holding blunt end of knife tip on board with one hand and moving blade up and down with the other hand.
- **Chill:** To make cold by refrigerating at least several hours.
- **Cool:** To allow to come to room temperature.
- **Cut in:** To distribute solid fat in dry ingredients by chopping with two knives or pastry blender.
- **Fold:** To combine ingredients, using an up-over-and-down motion with a wire whip or rubber spatula.
- **Dissolve:** To combine dry and liquid ingredients in solution.
- **Dough:** A mixture of flour, liquid and other ingredients; stiff enough to knead or roll.
- **Grate:** To cut into tiny particles, using small holes of grater, as with lemon peel, chocolate.
- **Knead:** To work dough into smooth and elastic mass, using pressing and folding motion of hands.
- **Mix:** To combine two or more ingredients until mixture is of uniform consistency.
- **Pare:** To cut off outer covering of apples, pears and other fruit and vegetables with a knife, parer or other sharp tool.
- **Peel:** To strip off outer covering, as with fruit.
- **Refrigerate:** To place in refrigerator and make cold.
- **Sift:** To put dry ingredients through a sieve or sifter.
- **Simmer:** To cook a liquid or in a liquid at a temperature just below boiling; bubbles form slowly and break below surface.
- **Sliver:** To cut into long thin pieces, as with almonds.
- **Stir:** To combine two or more ingredients with a circular or figure 8 motion until all ingredients are distributed evenly within mixture.
- **Toast:** To brown in oven or toaster, as with nuts or coconut.
- **Whip:** To beat rapidly to incorporate air, increase volume and make a fluffier mixture.

CHECK YOUR PANS

- A 10-inch Bundt® (fluted tube) pan and a 10-inch angel cake tube pan are *not* interchangeable; the Bundt® holds 12 cups of batter, the angel cake tube, 18 cups! Use a 9-inch angel cake tube pan as a substitute for Bundt®.
- For recipes using a 10-inch angel cake tube pan, you can use a 10-inch fluted tube pan, filling *only* two-thirds full, and pour remaining batter into an 8½ x 3⅝ x 2⅝-inch loaf pan.
- To determine amount of batter needed for odd-shaped pan, fill with

*Reprinted from Family Circle Great Ideas, January 1977.

1

measured water; use two-thirds that amount of batter.

• If you bake in glass pans, lower recipe temperature by 25°. Many new non-stick coated pans need a 25°-lower temperature, too—read label directions.

• Use heavy gauge metal pans for cake and cookie success.

• Cookie sheets should be at least 2 inches narrower than the oven.

• Always place cookie dough on cool baking sheet; it'll spread on hot one.

LINING PANS

• Line layer cake pans with wax paper for easier removal of delicate cakes.

• To give an even, golden crust to butter-type cakes, grease bottoms and sides of pans well with vegetable shortening, then dust with flour, shaking pan to coat well; tap out excess.

• Don't grease and flour foam cake pans. Cakes like angel food and chiffon have to cling to pan for rising.

• To grease cookie sheets, rub surface lightly with vegetable shortening. Don't grease sheets for cookies made with a cookie press.

ALL ABOUT FLOUR

• It isn't necessary to sift flour. Spoon it into a measuring cup, to overflowing (don't pack or tap), and level off at top with knife or spatula.

• Only use standard dry measures.

• Always make level measurements.

• Use all purpose flour for baking our recipes, unless otherwise specified.

• Whole wheat flour is generally too heavy for delicate baked goods. It contains the entire wheat grain, including bran, so use only in recipes calling for it.

• Unbleached white flour may be used in place of all purpose flour.

• Cake flour is milled from the highest grade soft wheat and suitable when you want a lighter product.

• To substitute all purpose flour for cake flour, remove 2 tablespoons from each cup of measured flour.

MEASURING DRY INGREDIENTS

Dash	= under	⅛ teaspoon
1 tablespoon	= 3	teaspoons
¼ cup	= 4	tablespoons
⅓ cup	= 5	tablespoons
	+ 1	teaspoon
½ cup	= 8	tablespoons
1 cup	= 16	tablespoons

HIGH ALTITUDE BAKING

• If you live less than 3,000 feet above sea level, you probably won't need to adjust recipes. Above that, follow the chart given below. Use small adjustment the first time you try a recipe; make larger adjustment only if necessary, or contact utility company.

Altitude (feet)	3,000-4,000	4,000-6,000	6,000-7,500
Reduce Baking Powder: For each teaspoon, decrease	⅛ tsp.	⅛-¼ tsp.	¼ tsp.
Reduce Sugar: For each cup, decrease	1 tbsp.	1-2 tbsp.	3-4 tbsp.
Increase Liquid: For each cup, add	1-2 tbsp.	2-4 tbsp.	3-4 tbsp.

• For all adjusted recipes, increase temperature 25°.

• For especially rich cakes, reduce the shortening by 1-2 tablespoons.

• For very high altitudes, increase the amount of egg in angel food, chiffon or sponge cakes.

(These are only general guides.)

CAKE BATTER

• Only fill a cake or cupcake tin ⅔ full with batter to allow for rising.

• To adapt recipes to pans of varied sizes, use those with same batter yield. Round pans:
- 6-inch pan holds 1 ¼ cups batter.
- 8-inch pan holds 2 ¼ cups batter.
- 9-inch pan holds 2 ½ cups batter.
- 10-inch pan holds 3 ⅔ cups batter.
- 11-inch pan holds 4 ¼ cups batter.
- 12-inch pan holds 5 ¾ cups batter.

Square pans:
- 8-inch pan holds 3 ½ cups batter.
- 10-inch pan holds 6 cups batter.
- 12-inch pan holds 9 cups batter.

Tube pans:
- 9-inch pan holds 5 cups batter.

COOLING CAKES AND COOKIES

• Cool "foam" cakes—for example, angel food, chiffon and sponge—upside down, over a funnel or one-quart bottle; the walls cool and strengthen enough to support themselves when cake is placed right-side up.
• Cool butter cakes on wire racks.
• With especially fragile cakes, line wire rack with clean cloth and invert cake onto wire rack; top with second wire rack, and turn cake right-side up.

THE PERFECT CUT

• To split a sponge tube cake, insert wooden picks evenly all around cake; use picks as guide for knife, always cutting toward center of cake with long, thin serrated knife; cut across and through.
• When slicing a sponge, angel or chiffon cake, use serrated knife or special cake breaker.
• For fruit cakes and heavy cakes, use sharp French knife.
• Dip knife in hot water and wipe with damp cloth or paper towel before slicing to prevent frosting from sticking to knife. Also helpful in cutting cheesecakes.
• Some cakes, such as tea breads and pound cakes, slice better the day after they're baked.

• Here's the number of servings you can expect to get from a cake:

9x5x3-inch loaf 8
8-inch square . . . . 8 or 9
9-inch square 9
8-inch double layer 10-12
9-inch double layer 12-16
13x9x2-inch 12-16
10-inch fluted or tube 10-12
10-inch jelly roll 10

• To keep a square double-layer cake from collapsing when you cut it, slice a quarter at a time.

STORING CAKES AND COOKIES

• To keep cookies crisp, store in container between layers of wax paper. Keep in cool place.
• To keep cookies soft, store in tin with an apple wedge or piece of soft white bread to add moixture, but replace them often.
• To freshen soft cookies, put in casserole, cover and bake at 300° for 8-10 minutes.
• To freshen crisp cookies before serving, place on baking sheet and heat at 300° for 3-5 minutes.
• For cakes with fluffy frosting, slip knife under cake carrier so it won't be airtight.
• For whipped cream frosting cakes, keep in refrigerator, covered with inverted bowl.
• Cakes with butter frostings may be loosely covered with foil or plastic wrap or stored in a cake carrier.

MAILING CAKES AND COOKIES

• Choose the right cakes and cookies for mailing: Soft drop, bar and fruit cookies mail well; fruit and pound cakes are good travelers, too.
• For cookies, use empty metal coffee or shortening tins; cakes may be sent in strong cardboard boxes.
• Wrap cookies in pairs, flat sides to-

gether, with foil and seal with cellophane tape; use plastic wrap, then foil, for cakes.
• Use crumpled foil, wax paper, or shredded tissue paper to line bottom and top of container and fill in any spaces; shifting causes breakage.
• Wrap container in corrugated cardboard, then double layer of brown paper; tie with twine or heavy string; label on one side only, using the words, "Perishable" and "Fragile" and "Handle with Care."

FREEZING CAKES AND COOKIES

Freezing Cakes:
• Unfrosted cakes freeze best—up to 4 months. Wrap in aluminum foil, plastic wrap, or large plastic bags; thaw at room temperature 1 hour.
• Frosted cakes should be frozen on piece of cardboard or a cookie sheet until firm, then wrapped in aluminum foil, plastic wrap or very large plastic bags; freeze up to 3 months and thaw at room temperature 2 hours.
Freezing cookies:
• Both dough and baked cookies can be frozen and stored for 9-12 months.
• Baked cookies should be frozen in strong box lines with plastic wrap or foil; separate each layer with more wrap or

foil; thaw cookies at room temperature 10 minutes.
• Cookie dough may be frozen in foil or plastic wrap.
• Drop cookie dough should be thawed until just soft enough to use.
• Refrigerator cookie rolls should be thawed just enough to slice.
• Rolled cookies can be frozen already shaped; place, still frozen, onto cookie sheets.
• Freeze bar cookie dough in pan in which it is to be baked; cover with plastic wrap, then foil.

DON'T DISCARD LEFTOVERS

Cake and cookie crumbs can be used in many creative ways.
• Use them to roll around ice cream balls, then top with your favorite chocolate or butterscotch sauce.
• Moisten cake pieces with fruit juice, sweetened coffee, sherry or your favorite liqueur; fold into pudding, or serve topped with cream, whipped or just plain.
• Make crumb crusts for cream pies from leftover cookies.
• Use crushed cookies as a topping for puddings, fruit crisps, fruit cups or ice cream.

WINES OF CALIFORNIA

by
JIM WIECHERS

Jim Wiechers, on the PGA Tour for 10 years; winner, West End Classic, 1969; $315,000 career earnings; 32 years old, wife, Susan; daughter, Erica, 7 years. He was Lee Elder's caddy during playoff of 1974 Pensacola Open. Wiechers is a Napa Valley, Cal. resident and wine taster extrordinair. He is also co-owner of August L. Casazza, Inc., wine importers and wholesalers.

The many wine growing areas of California, primarily those in the North, are climatically the finest in the world. The consistently wet, warm springs and hot, dry summers are a winemakers dream. Additionally, the fertile valleys and rocky hillsides make it possible to grow successfully, almost all of the world's great grape varieties. These two factors, plus the technology developed at the worlds finest school of viticulture and enology (Univ. of California at Davis) makes the wines of California some of the greatest known to man.

The wines of California are divided into two categories: Generic and Varietal. Generic wines are generally a blend of many grape varieties and are identified by the wine region of the world they most closely resemble. E.g. Burgundy, Chablis, Rhine, Claret. Varietal wines are identified by the specific grape variety used in producing the wine e.g. Cabernet Savingnon, Pinot Chardonnay, Pinot Noir, Grey Reishing, etc. Varietal wines must contain 51% of the grape after which it is named. This is a minimum and generally the winemaker will use 80, 90, and sometimes 100 percent of the grape variety.

Now that you have a brief idea of the whys and whats of California wines, I will try to list some of the better wines and wineries of which we Californians are proud.

The wines with which most people are familiar are the jug wines. These are mostly generic wines and are so called because they come in screw-top half gallons or gallons. Though this type wine is generally of low quality and cost, there are a few real bargains to be found. Gallo Vineyards, which makes 40% of the wine consumed in the U.S., has an excellent bargain in their *Hearty Burgundy*. Their *Chablis Blanc* is a fine everyday wine, which is easily stored in the refrigerator for whenever the need for a white wine arises. The Mountain Reds, Whites and Rosés of Louis Martini are another example that jug wines are not all that bad. Usually, a jug wine made by a vintner known for his varietal wines is made from his own high quality grapes and therefore a pleasant tasting wine at a reasonable price. Buying a jug wine made by these wineries is a pretty good rule of thumb to follow.

For those people whose taste in wines is a bit more sophisticated, California offers some of the world's finest varieties. The world famous Cabenet gets no finer treatment anywhere in the world than in California. The recent vintages such as *Robert Monoavi's* 1969 C.S., Beaulieu 1970 Private Reserve, and Heitz Cellars 1968 Martha's Vineyard, have matched and in many cases surpassed the Chateau Lafittes, Margaux, Latovas, etc. in wine tasting around the world. Unfortunately most of these great vintages are snatched up by knowledgeable wine drinkers and are rarely seen outside California. Although most people may never see a great David Bruce *Cabernet*, there are many other California varietals that are sold most everywhere in the U.S. The varietal reds of the forementioned Louis Martini; of Christian Brothers, Inglenook, Charles Krug, Beringer, Sebastiani or Beaulieu's regular vintages are of excellent quality and in many individual cases as good as you'll ever want to taste.

In the varietal whites, the king is the Pinot Chardonnay. Unfortunately the better Pinot's of California are these days being made by such small wineries as *Chateau Montelena, Spring Mountain, Thetz Cellars, Freemark Abbey* and *Sterling Vineyards*. There are, however, two fine Pinot Chardonnays that are normally found around the country, *Robert Mondain* and *Wente Brothers*. Though the Pinot Chardonnays are hard to find, there are fortunately many other California white varietals to be found everywhere, being of varying tastes to satisfy anybody's palate. If you prefer a sweeter white wine, try a Chenin Clanc or a late harvest Reisling. For a dryer, spicier wine try a Johannesberg Reisling or a French Columbard. If you like something dry, yet fruity, that's a well made Pinot Chardonnay or Fume Blanc. The wineries to look for: Wente Brothers, Christian Brothers, Mirasson, Concannon, and Weibel, just to name a few.

The last type of wine I will cover will be the Rosé's. Unfortunately, not too many varietal rosés are made, but two I can recommend, one sweet and one dry, should not be to hard to find. The dryer one *Robert Mondavi* Gamay Rosé is a personal favorite and a great luncheon wine. The sweeter rosé, *Sabastiani* Grenache Rosé, is a great one for the gals (girls, not gallons).

Unfortunately, time and space prevents me from going deeply into the many other varieties of wine such as champagnes, ports, aperitifs, etc. but I'll quickly mention Schramberg Champagne if it can be found.

California wines are of special quality and for all tastes and pocketbooks. I hope I have mentioned one that you can find and enjoy. If not, don't be disillusioned for there are many, many other California wines sitting on the shelves of stores all over the country just waiting to make your meal more enjoyable.

In closing, I will ask you to remember one important ingredient in wine tasting: The best wine in the world is the one you most enjoy—just make it Californian.

I

Appetizers & First Courses

Editor's Note

THE FIRST COURSE

Hors d'oeuvres, the French word that is also understood by all in English is something to be served before the meal. For French families this is usually a daily routine. In America more simple hors d'oeuvres such as vegetables, pickles, olives, etc. are often used as a pre-cocktails repast, unless we want to add more substance to a meal.

IRENE REAVES (CALVIN)

Little Meat Balls in Tomato Sauce

(meat balls)

1½ lbs. ground beef
1 medium onion, grated
⅓ cup chopped parsley
1 egg, unbeaten
1 slice bread, coarsely crumbled
¾ tsp. salt
dash of pepper
¼ tsp. marjoram

(tomato sauce)

2 cans (8 oz.) tomato sauce
1 small onion, grated
dash of curry powder
dash of ground cloves
¼ tsp. salt

1 Combine meat ball ingredients in large mixing bowl.
2 In large sauce pan mix ingredients for sauce and bring to boil, stir often. Turn off heat.
3 Form beef mixture lightly into bite size balls, drop each into sauce.
4 Reheat sauce to boiling and simmer meat balls over low heat for 5 minutes or to desired doneness stirring occasionally.
5 Serve meat balls in sauce with savory rice, piping hot.

MARY HARRIS (LABRON)

Spinach Balls

2 10 oz. packages frozen
  spinach, cooked and
  well drained
2 cups packaged stuffing mix
1 cup grated Parmesan cheese

6 eggs, beaten
¾ cup butter, softened
salt and pepper

1 In large mixing bowl, combine all the ingredients, mixing well.
2 Roll into balls the size of walnuts.
3 Freeze balls preferably on a cookie sheet to retain shape.
4 Before serving, bake frozen balls (cookie sheet can go directly from freezer to oven) for 10 minutes at 350°. Makes 60-70 balls.

PATTY CLARKE (BUDDY)

Quiche Lorraine

1 tbs. chives, chopped
3 eggs, lightly beaten
1 cup light cream
5 slices crisp bacon, crumbled
3 tbs. Dijon mustard
1 cup onion, finely minced

1 cup grated Swiss cheese
¼ tsp. salt
⅛ tsp. pepper
dash Worcestershire
1 9-inch pie shell, unbaked

1 Combine all the ingredients and pour into the pie shell.
2 Bake in preheated 375° oven for 35-40 minutes, or until an inserted knife comes out clean. Serves 4-6.

*"Buddy says the mustard is the secret. It's
sharp and intimately delicious."*

ROSE ELDER (LEE)

Eggplant

1 eggplant
1 cup all purpose flour
1 cup ice water
1 egg, slightly beaten
2 tbs. cooking oil

½ tsp. sugar
½ tsp. Season All
½ tsp. Accent
grated Parmesan cheese

1 Cut eggplant in half, lengthwise. Then cut into ½ inch thick slices. Then cut slices into ½ inch strips.
2 Beat flour, water, egg, oil, sugar and Season All together.
3 Dip eggplant in batter. Allow excess batter to drain off.
4 Fry a few slices at a time in deep hot fat for 4 or 5 minutes.
5 Drain on paper towel. Sprinkle with more Season All. Serve with Parmesan cheese.

*"I personally like a garlic flavor. Instead of additional
Season All, I sprinkle lightly with garlic salt."*

SALLIE BROWN (ROBERT)

Bob's Famous Open Faced Sandwich

English muffin, sliced in half
mayonnaise
lettuce
2 slices onion

2 slices tomato
2 slices boiled ham
several canned asparagus spears
2 slices Provalone cheese

1 Set oven to broil.

2 Spread each half of muffin with mayonnaise and layer each with lettuce, onions, tomatoes, ham, asparagus, and cheese.

3 Place open sandwich on flat baking sheet. Broil until cheese melts. Serve immediately.

JEAN POHANKA (JACK)

Breakfast Crepes

⅔ cup flour
2 tbs. sugar
¼ tsp. salt
3 eggs

1¾ cup milk
2 tbs. flavoring (grand maniere,
    cognac, rum, cointreau, or
    whathaveyou); more or less to taste

1 Mix together flour, sugar and salt. Add eggs and mix well with a wire whisk. Add milk and flavoring. Mix altogether until smooth. Strain through a fine sieve.

2 Put butter in a hot skillet, using just enough to grease it. When very hot, pour in just enough batter to cover the bottom of the skillet thinly.

3 When set and starting to brown on the underside, turn over and cook until done. (Iron skillets do the best job. For breakfast crepes, a larger skillet than normal crepe size may be used. Also, using two skillets, flipping from one to another, speeds production.)

4 Put in a hot serving dish and sprinkle with powdered sugar. Spread with marmalade or jelly and roll up. Makes 12 to 15 pancakes, depending on size of skillet.

> "If you would rather sleep under an electric blanket
> than under several regular blankets, you'll prefer
> these breakfast crepes to pancakes!"

HELEN MURCH

Hot Dip

1 cup sour cream
1 3-oz. pkg. dried beef,
   or 1 glass jar
dash of pepper

1 8-oz. pkg. cream cheese
½ tsp. garlic salt
½ tsp. onion salt
½ cup chopped nuts

1 *Beat cream cheese and sour cream until light and fluffy.*
2 *Stir in beef and seasonings.*
3 *Place in shallow baking dish. Top with nuts. Bake at 350° for 20 minutes. Good cold the next day.*

ROSE ELDER (LEE)

Fruit or Vegetable Fritters

1 egg
1 tsp. Accent
1 tsp. Season All
2 cups fruit or cooked vegetables

2 cups Bisquick
⅔ cup milk
1 tsp. sugar

1 *Mix well: Bisquick, milk, egg, Accent, Season All and sugar in large mixing bowl.*
2 *Stir in fruit or vegetables (if canned, be sure to drain well).*
3 *Drop by small teaspoonful into deep hot oil in large skillet or deep fryer and fry until golden brown on both sides.*
4 *Drain on paper towel.*
5 *Roll in powdered sugar or cinnamon sugar. Yields about 2 dozen.*

ROSE ELDER (LEE)

Guacamole

4 large avocados, peeled & diced
2 hard boiled eggs, chopped
1 medium sized tomato, chopped
1 medium sized onion, grated
1 tsp. Season All

½ tsp. garlic salt
2 tbs. lemon juice
dash Tabasco, or to taste
1 avocado, peeled & sliced
1 head lettuce

1 *Combine all ingredients except avocado slices. Toss lightly, being careful not to bruise avocados. Serve on bed of lettuce.*

2 *Garnish with avocado slices.*

MARILYN DERMER (HAROLD)

Chopped Liver

1 lb. chicken livers,
   broiled and finely chopped
3 to 4 eggs, hard boiled
   and finely chopped

two large onions, diced fine
chicken fat
salt to taste

1 *In mixing bowl, combine all ingredients.*

2 *Add chicken fat until you get a palatable taste.*

3 *Add salt to taste and serve.*

MARILYN DERMER (HAROLD)

Pickled Fish

2 large onions, sliced
1 lb. trout, sliced with bones
1 tbs. salt
1 tsp. or less pickling spices

2 dashes pepper
½ tbs. sugar (or to taste)
¾ cup vinegar
¼ cup water

1 *Place all ingredients in a large pot. Cover and refrigerate over night.*

2 *In the morning boil for 30 minutes.*

3 *Cool slightly and place in glass dish. Refrigerate to jell. Serve as appetizer or main dish.*

ROSE ELDER (LEE)

Boiled Mushrooms with Cream

3 tbs. margarine or butter
1 lb. mushrooms, sliced
¼ cup shallots

1 cup whipping cream
2 tbs. parsley, minced
Season Salt, to taste
dash of white pepper

1 Simmer mushrooms, margarine, shallots and cup of whipping cream in a wide frying pan over a low to medium heat for 5-7 minutes, stirring occasionally.

2 Then turn up heat to high, and boil uncovered, stirring frequently for about 10 more minutes. Liquid will reduce to a shiny sauce and bubbles will form.

3 Stir in parsley, Season Salt and pepper. Yields 4 regular servings or 6 appetizers.

ROSE ELDER (LEE)

Hot Asparagus Rolls

1 loaf sandwich bread,
   thinly sliced
Season All
1 lb. fresh asparagus spears,
   cooked

¼ cup soft butter or margarine
¼ cup mayonnaise
½ cup capers

1 Trim crust from sandwich slices.

2 Spread with butter or margarine, and then with mayonnaise. Sprinkle with Season All and a few capers.

3 Roll each bread slice around one drained asparagus spear.

4 Chill until time for serving, then bake at 400° for 15 minutes. If necessary, turn to brown both sides.

II

Beverages

Editor's Note

BEVERAGES

When in France, I noted that the matching of food and wine is taken very seriously when having formal meals. However, it is common knowledge that one should observe his own personal taste when choosing the wine. Usually, a Frenchman will have any kind of wine as opposed to none. While visiting a few homes, there was always both red and white wine on the table, regardless of the main course.

Art Spandler (a writer for a San Francisco newspaper, when interviewing Lee in Palm Springs at the Bob Hope Classic) made mention of the fact that Lee Elder was having "Blue Nun" with his steak. . . . (It's ok Art, the French do it too.)

Americans are fortunate to have some of the finest wines right here at home, and many of us find ourselves enjoying more and more domestic wines. Our good friend Jim Wiechers tells us about the "Wines of California" elsewhere in this book.

MIRIAM BEMAN (DEANE)

Rum Punch

4 tea bags
2 cups boiling water
1 cup sugar (dissolved in
    ½ cup heated water)
juice from 3-4 large lemons
1½ 16 oz. cans pineapple
    chunks and juice

1 tsp. vanilla
1 tsp. almond extract
1½ qts. ginger ale
½ qt. club soda
1 fifth light rum

1 *Steep tea in boiling water for 10 minutes.*
2 *Mix together tea, dissolved sugar, and lemon juice.*
3 *Cool to room temperature.*
4 *Add rest of ingredients, stirring well. Serve cold. Makes 40 cups.*

ROSE ELDER (LEE)

Bull Shot

1 can condensed beef broth,
    undiluted (10 oz.)
½ can water

1 tsp. Worcestershire sauce
½ cup vodka (Smirnoff 80)

1 *Mix all ingredients together in shaker or jar. Shake well.*
2 *Serve over ice with stick of celery in highball glasses. May be·served hot or cold.*

ROSE ELDER (LEE)

Champagne Punch

1 bottle champagne
1 qt. fresh strawberries
1 bottle Johannesberg Rhine
1 shot cognac or brandy

½ pt. club soda
½ pt. tonic water
juice of half lemon

1 *Place strawberries in punch bowl, add lemon juice, shot of cognac, and ½ the bottle of wine.*

2 *Let stand in refrigerator for about 2 hours.*

3 *When ready to serve, add good size chunks of ice and rest of ingredients. Stir slightly. Serves 8-10 people.*

Note: An added attraction—freeze fresh mint in ice.

ROSE ELDER (LEE)

Coffee Punch

½ cup boiling water
½ cup sugar
2 tbs. instant coffee or Sanka
1 pt. chocolate ice cream
   (cut into chunks)

3½ cups milk
½ pt. whipped cream
1 tbs. Amaretto liqueur
   (or ¼ tsp. almond flavoring)

1 *Combine boiling water, coffee and sugar and let cool.*

2 *Add cold milk to cooled coffee.*

3 *When ready to serve add Amaretto liqueur and fold in whipped cream and ice cream chunks to taste.*

III

Breads

Editor's Note

BREADS

*When in Paris it always amazed me to see
Frenchmen going to the (Boulangerie) bakery
for breads. You see many children with long
loaves of bread under their arms (not wrapped
like in the States). While there, I asked the
French people about this. Many told me it was a
habit and a carryover from old days when the
bakers were the only ones with good ovens.
However, now they say it's a convenience, they
always have fresh breads. One of my favorites
in France is the croissants.*

VIVA SMITH

Mexican Cornbread

2 pkgs. (8 oz. size) corn
  muffin mix
2 eggs
2 cartons (8 oz. size) sour cream
1 tsp. soda

1 cup cream corn
1 cup grated sharp cheddar cheese
6 Jalapena peppers, seeded and
  chopped fine (1 small jar)

1 *Mix together muffin mix, eggs, sour cream, soda, cream corn.*

2 *Pour half of the batter into a greased baking pan; add half of the cheese and all of the peppers. Add remaining batter and cheese on top.*

3 *Bake at 375° for 45 minutes.*

NANCY SNEED (ED)

Oatmeal Bread

6 cups flour, unbleached
2 tsp. salt
2 tbs. soft butter
½ cup honey

1 cup rolled oats
2 cups boiling water
2 pkg. active dry yeast
⅓ cup warm water (120°)

1 *Place oats in large mixing bowl and pour boiling water over. Let set in bowl until temperature of oats is 110-120°. When oats have reached 120°, dissolve yeast in ⅓ cup warm water.*

2 *Add salt, honey and butter to oats and stir well. Add yeast; stir well again. Add 4 cups flour, stirring well after each two cups. Knead in last 2 cups for about 10 minutes.*

3 *Shape in bowl. Cover with greased waxed paper and a damp dish towel. Let rise until double (about 1 hour). Punch down. Divide into two loaves.*

4 *Place in well greased pans 9 x 5 x 3 inches. Let rise until double. Bake 40-50 minutes at 325° four inches from bottom of oven. Cool on wire racks.*

SIS GOEKEN (DICK)

Cornbread Dressing

1½ cups yellow cornmeal
½ cup flour
4 tsp. baking powder
1 tbs. sugar
1 ½ cups milk
3 eggs
4 stalks chopped celery
2 tbs. oil

2 bunches chopped green onions
1 small button garlic, chopped
1 stick butter
6 chicken bouillon cubes
1 tsp. oregano
1 tsp. sage
1 tbs. dried parsley

1 *Mix well, cornmeal, flour, baking powder, sugar, milk and 1 egg.*
2 *Pour batter into hot skillet that is coated with 2 tbs. oil and bake at 450° for 25 minutes.*
3 *Saute celery, onions, and garlic in 1 stick butter until tender. Add chicken bouillon cubes, oregano, sage, and parsley.*
4 *In separate dish, crumble cornbread. Add sauteed mixture and the other two eggs. Mix well.*
5 *Put in buttered baking dish and bake at 375° for 1½ hours.*

"Great to make a day ahead"

SCOTTY SANDERS (DOUG)

Corn Bread

1 cup corn meal
¼ cup wheat flour
1 tsp. baking powder
½ tsp. salt

1 egg, beaten
½ cup milk
1 tbs. melted butter

1 *Sift together dry ingredients in large mixing bowl.*
2 *In separate dish, combine milk and egg then add to dry ingredients.*
3 *Add melted butter and mix well.*
4 *Pour batter into a well-greased pan and bake in hot oven at 425° for 25 minutes.*

SUSAN NORTH (ANDY)

Caramel Rolls

⅓ cup melted butter
⅓ cup sugar
2 eggs, beaten
1½ tsp. salt

1½ cup scalded milk, cooled
1 pkg. dry yeast
½ cup warm water
6 cups flour

1 *Dissolve yeast in ½ cup warm water.*
2 *In large mixing bowl, add butter, sugar, eggs, salt, milk and yeast mixture to flour. Mix thoroughly and knead about eight times.*
3 *Place in greased bowl to rise until about double its size (about 1 hour). Then punch down dough and let rise again.*
4 *Roll out to about ½ inch thickness and spread with melted butter and brown sugar.*
5 *Sprinkle bottom of 2 baking pans with brown sugar and sprinkle cinnamon over flattened dough.*
6 *Roll up dough and slice in one inch slices.*
7 *Place in pans and spread with a little melted butter.*
8 *Let rise and bake at 375° for 20-25 minutes.*

NOEL BLANCAS (HOMERO)

Cinnamon Sticks

1 loaf day-old potato bread
  or coarse bread
½ lb. butter, melted

¼ cup cinnamon
¾ cup sugar

1 *Cut crust from loaf of bread. Cut bread into 1-inch slices and each slice into thirds.*
2 *Melt butter in small sauce pan.*
3 *Mix cinnamon and sugar in small bowl.*
4 *Dip bread strips into melted butter and then into sugar and cinnamon mixture.*
5 *Place bread strips in shallow baking pan and bake at 375° for 15 minutes.*

TALLY MARR (DAVE)

Fancy Garlic Bread

½ lb. butter, melted
¼ cup fresh parsley, chopped
¼ cup Parmesan cheese

1 small button garlic, minced
1 loaf French bread, sliced

1 Cut bread into 1-inch slices.
2 Melt butter and add chopped fresh parsley and minced garlic.
3 Brush butter on slices and cover generously with Parmesan cheese.
4 Toast slices in shallow baking pan in 375° oven for 15 minutes.

CLAUDIA ROBINSON

Pumpkin Bread

4 eggs
2¾ cups sugar
⅔ cup water
1 cup Crisco oil
1 can pumpkin
3½ cups flour

2 tsp. baking soda
1 tsp. salt
1 tsp. nutmeg
1 tsp. cinnamon
½ cup nuts

1 Beat eggs in large mixing bowl. Add sugar, pumpkin, oil and water and mix well. Add the dry ingredients and mix well again.
2 Place into two loaf pans that have been greased and floured.
3 Bake at 325° for ½ hour.
4 Reduce heat to 300° and bake for 45 minutes longer or until bread leaves side of pan.

*"I make this each week during the summer. I
have yet to find a golfer or anyone who didn't
enjoy it. This can be frozen for weeks ahead,
so it works in grand for busy, busy folks."*

LINDA TOEPEL (JOHN)

Easy Refrigerator Rolls

1 pkg. yeast
1 cup warm water
¼ cup sugar
⅛ to ¼ cup butter, softened

1 tsp. salt
1 egg
3¼ to 3½ cup flour

1 *Dissolve yeast in warm water.*
2 *Stir in sugar, salt, butter and egg. Mix in flour until dough is easy to handle.*
3 *Place in greased bowl. Cover with cloth and place in refrigerator.*
4 *About 2 hours before baking, knead.*
5 *Cover again and let rise at room temperature until double in size (1½ to 2 hours.*
6 *Shape into rolls and bake at 400° for 12 to 15 minutes.*

VIVIENNE PLAYER (GARY)

Brown Bread

1 tsp. brown sugar
9 cups brown wholewheat flour
2 tbs. dry yeast

2 tbs. honey, melted
2 tsp. salt
¼ lb. margarine

1 *In separate container add dry yeast, brown sugar and one cup lukewarm water; set aside to rise for 15 min.*
2 *Mix flour, salt, melted honey and margarine together with 3 cups warm water.*
3 *Combine yeast mixture which will be a very thick dough.*
4 *Cover and allow to rise in a warm place for 45 minutes.*
5 *Divide into 3 baking tins, well greased.*
6 *Bake in 400° oven for one hour. Yields 3 small loaves.*

JANA HAYES (MARK)

Dilly Casserole Bread

1 pkg. yeast
¼ cup warm water
1 cup creamed cottage cheese,
   heated to luke warm
2 tbs. sugar or honey
1 tbs. minced onion

1 tbs. butter
2 tsp. dill seed
1 tsp. salt
¼ tsp. soda
1 unbeaten egg
2¼-2½ cups flour (use equal
   parts unbleached white and
   wholewheat flour for richer
   taste)

1 Soften yeast in water.

2 Combine in large mixing bowl: cottage cheese, sugar, onion, butter, dill seed, salt, soda, egg and softened yeast.

3 Add flour to form a stiff dough, beating well after each addition (for first addition, use mixer on low speed).

4 Cover and let rise in warm place 50-60 minutes until doubled in size. Stir down dough. Turn into well greased 8-inch round casserole dish (1½ or 2-qt. dish). Let rise again for 30-40 minutes.

5 Bake at 350°, 40-50 minutes until golden brown. Brush baked loaf with butter and sprinkle with salt.

IWALANI RODRIGUEZ (CHI CHI)

Mango Bread

4 cups flour
4 tsp. soda
4 tsp. cinnamon
1 tsp. salt
½ cup chopped walnuts
2½ cups oil

2 tsp. vanilla
3 cups sugar
4 cups diced mangoes
6 eggs
1 cup seedless raisins
1 cup coconut (optional)

1 Sift dry ingredients together. Make a well with the dry ingredients (well is a hole in center) and add the rest.

2 Mix lightly. Pour into two well greased loaf pans. Bake 1 hour at 350°.

JANIE JONES (GRIER)

Bran Muffins

1½ cup sugar
½ cup shortening
2 eggs
2½ tsp. soda
½ tsp. salt

1 cup buttermilk
1 cup boiling water
1 cup 100% Bran (ready to eat cereal)
2 cups All Bran (ready to eat cereal)

1 *Cream together sugar and shortening.*

2 *Add eggs one at a time. Mix well after each addition.*

3 *Add flour, soda, salt, buttermilk; mix until smooth.*

4 *Pour boiling water over 100% Bran and let stand until absorbed and cooled slightly. Blend into batter. Add All Bran. Mix thoroughly.*

5 *Bake for 20 minutes at 400°. Recipe may be doubled or made 1½ times.*

   Can be refrigerated covered up to 5 weeks. Don't stir when putting into muffin tin.

ROSE ELDER (LEE)

Cheese and Sausage Biscuits

1 lb. hot chopped Italian sausage
½ lb. grated sharp cheddar cheese

3½ cups Bisquick mix
1 tsp. Season All

1 *Cook sausage in skillet until well done. Do not overcook.*

2 *Drain off fat and add cheese stirring well to blend.*

3 *Add Bisquick mix and Season All and mix well again.*

4 *Form into small balls and place on oiled cookie sheet. Flatten out slightly. Bake in 375° oven for 12-15 minutes. Serve hot.*

"Great for brunch with salad and wine."

ROSE ELDER (LEE)

Lavosh

1 lb. bread flour	¼ oz. salt
2 cups milk	¼ oz. sugar
2 whole eggs	2 oz. shortening
	sesame seeds

1 *Mix all ingredients well into a solid dough and leave for one hour.*
2 *Roll dough on floured board with sesame seeds, as thin as possible.*
3 *Put on floured sheet pan. Bake in steam oven at 400° for 5 minutes or bake without steam until brown at 350°. Enough for 2 sheets.*

VIVIENNE PLAYER (GARY)

Honey Wholewheat Bread

2 tsp. dry yeast	4 tsp. salt
1 tsp. sugar	2 oz. butter
½ cup warm water	2 tbs. honey
9 cups nutty wheat flour	warm water to mix

1 *Dissolve yeast in ½ cup warm water with sugar—put in warm place to rise.*
2 *Melt butter and honey together.*
3 *In large mixing bowl, place flour, salt, and add yeast mixture (when risen); add butter and honey mixture.*
4 *Add just enough warm water to make a thick stiff dough.*
5 *Divide into three small bread tins, leave to rise in warm place.*
6 *Bake in preheated oven at 400° for one hour.*

"Trial and error is the best as far as the water goes—also, one can experiment with different types of whole wheat flour. I also sprinkle sesame seeds on top before baking."

RACHEL WADKINS (LANNY)

Angel Biscuits

2 cups buttermilk
1 pkg. dry yeast
2 tsp. lukewarm water
1 tsp. soda
5 cups flour

3 tsp. baking powder
4 tbs. sugar
1 tsp. salt
1 cup shortening (part oleo)

1 *Dissolve yeast in lukewarm water and set aside.*

2 *Mix soda, flour, baking powder, sugar and salt.*

3 *Blend shortening (part oleo) into flour mix.*

4 *Add buttermilk and dissolved yeast.*

5 *Mix with fork and then knead on floured board about 10 times.*

6 *Roll out about ¼ inch thick and cut with biscuit cutter.*

7 *Bake in 400° oven about 15 to 20 minutes.*

ROSE ELDER (LEE)

Yorkshire Pudding to Serve with Roast Beef

1 cup milk
1 cup flour
2 eggs, slightly beaten

¼ tsp. Season All
dash Accent

1 *Mix Season All, Accent and flour and gradually add milk to form a smooth paste. Add eggs.*

2 *Cover bottom of hot pan with some of beef fat from your roast and pour mixture into pan ½ inch deep. (Optional, can be done in muffin pan).*

3 *Bake for 20 minutes in hot oven, 375°, and baste with fat after pudding has risen.*

DIANNE CRAWFORD (RICHARD)

Refrigerator Yeast Biscuits

2½ cups lukewarm water
½ cup sugar
1½ tsp. salt
½ cup shortening, melted

2 pkg. yeast
2 eggs
4 cups flour (in tray for kneading)
4-5 cups flour, sifted

1 *In large mixing bowl dissolve yeast in water.*
2 *Add other ingredients, mixing in enough flour to make medium soft dough and mix well.*
3 *Place in floured kneading tray and knead until velvety.*
4 *Place in well greased large container.*
5 *Cover and let rise until double in size (about one hour).*
6 *Knead down and make into biscuits or place in refrigerator in covered container. Keep in refrigerator for a week. Cook on greased pan at 350° for 12-15 minutes.*

IV

Desserts & Cookies

AL ROBERTO

(Given to Rose Elder)

Cheesecake

(crust)
1 pkg. graham crackers,
   crushed (approx. 1¼ cups)
¼ cup sugar
¼ cup butter or margarine

(cake)
3 large pkgs. cream cheese
   (8 oz.)
5 eggs
1 tsp. vanilla
1 cup sugar

(topping)
1 pt. sour cream
½ cup sugar
1 tsp. vanilla

1 *Mix well crust ingredients and press into large pie plate (10 inches or larger). Set aside.*

2 *Using cake ingredients, cream the cream cheese. Add eggs, one at a time, then add vanilla and sugar.*

3 *Mix together thoroughly and pour into crust. Bake one hour at 325˚.*

4 *Make topping by blending all ingredients together. Take cake from oven and pour topping over. Return to oven for 5 minutes at 475˚.*

BETTY ALTOMONTE (JOE)

Hot Fruit Compote

3 small cans apricots
3 small cans pineapple chunks
3 small cans peaches
3 #2 cans bing cherries

3 oranges
3 lemons
½ cup light brown sugar

1 *Grate rind of oranges and lemons into sugar.*

2 *Spread fruit layer by layer in a 9 x 13 inch baking dish, sprinkling each layer with brown sugar and nutmeg.*

3 *Slice oranges and lemons very thickly and layer on top. Then, sprinkle with brown sugar and nutmeg.*

4 *Bake at 350˚ for ½ hour. Serve with sour cream. Serves 6.*

MONICA TERRY
(Rose Elder's Godchild)

Crazy Cake

4 eggs
1 box yellow cake mix
¾ cup oil

¾ cup water
3¼ oz. instant pudding mix

1 *Mix all ingredients together until everything is moistened.*
2 *Beat by hand for 1½ minutes.*
3 *Pour into bundt or tube pan and bake for 40 to 45 minutes at 475°. Let cool, glaze or frost.*

   (Glaze: Mix fresh fruit juice with confectionary sugar to a glaze consistency.)

Coconut Crazy Cake

1 *Add ½ of an 8 oz. can of coconut to "ready to spread" vanilla frosting.*
2 *Add ½ of an 8 oz. can of coconut to the already mixed batter and blend. Bake as directed. Frost with prepared frosting when cake is cool.*

WALTER PITTS

Pecan Pie

8-inch pie crust
4 eggs, well beaten
1 cup white Karo syrup
1 cup dark Karo syrup
½ cup brown sugar
½ cup white granulated sugar
½ stick butter, melted

½ cup pecans, chopped
½ cup pecans, whole (to decorate)
1 tsp. flour
1 tsp. vanilla extract
1 tsp. brandy extract
1 jigger brandy

1 *Preheat oven to 375°.*
2 *Put all ingredients except whole pecans in mixing bowl and mix well. Pour into pie shell.*
3 *Place whole pecans on top to decorate. Place in oven about 45 minutes or until pie is firm.*

ZXLEMA PRICE

Pecan Cake

6 eggs, separated
3 cups sugar
1 cup butter
4½ cups cake flour or
   4 cups plain flour
3½ cups chopped pecans

2 tbs. black molasses
1 cup bourbon whiskey
1¼ tsp. baking powder
⅝ tsp. soda
dash nutmeg

1 *Preheat oven to 350°. Grease and flour 9 x 13-inch baking pan.*

2 *Flour pecans lightly and set aside.*

3 *Sift together flour, baking powder, baking soda, nutmeg.*

4 *Separate eggs.*

5 *Cream butter until light. Add sugar gradually. Add molasses, bourbon and egg yolks a little at a time alternating with sifted dry ingredients. Blend thoroughly after each addition.*

6 *Whip egg whites until stiff. Fold into above mixture until blended. Add pecans, stirring well until incorporated.*

7 *Pour into prepared pan. Bake 45 minutes or until cake tests done. Allow to cool in pan. Cut into squares. Serve plain or with your favorite topping.*

ROSE ELDER (LEE)

Rose's Fruit Delight With Galliano

1 can crushed pineapple (16 oz.)
1 can fruit cocktail (16 oz.)
1 can mandarin oranges (16 oz.)
1 pkg. miniature marshmallows
   (5½ oz.)

1 pkg. fresh coconut (7 oz.)
½ cup chopped pecans (optional)
1 cup sour cream (optional)
¼ cup Galliano (2 oz.)

1 *Drain all fruit and mix together all ingredients well.*

2 *Chill and serve in fruit cups. Serves 10-12.*

*"To garnish, this looks great on your table or buffet
with bunches of parsley around and orange halves cut
with diamond edges on top of salad."*

SIS GOEKEN (DICK)

Ambrosia Cake

½ cup butter
2 cups sugar
1 cup buttermilk
2 tsp. baking soda
3 beaten eggs
½ cup hot water

1 apple, chopped
3 cups flour
1 tsp. nutmeg
½ tsp. cloves
2 tsp. cocoa

1 Preheat oven to 350°.
2 Grease and flour three cake pans.
3 Sift flour and spices together. Add soda to buttermilk.
4 Cream butter and sugar. Add beaten eggs. Add flour and buttermilk mixtures alternately to egg mixture.
5 Mix cocoa and hot water and add to batter.
6 Fold in finely chopped apple.
7 Distribute batter evenly in the three pans. Bake 30 minutes. Cook and fill.

Filling

3 cups sugar
2 cups milk
¼ cup butter
1 grated orange

1 can grated coconut
1 small can crushed pineapple, drained
1 cup broken pecans
1 tsp. vanilla

1 In a large saucepan melt butter. Add sugar, milk and grated orange rind.
2 While stirring, cook until mixture forms a soft ball when dropped in cold water.
3 Beat until slightly stiff. Then add coconut, pineapple, pecans and vanilla.
4 Spread between cooled layers of cake. Serve.

VIRGINIA IVERSON (DON)

Apple Rumdum Cake

1 cup sugar	1 egg
¼ cup shortening	1 tsp. cinnamon
1 tsp. baking soda	2 cups diced apples
1 cup flour	

1 *Preheat oven to 350°.*

2 *Grease and flour 9 x 13-inch pan.*

3 *Place sugar, soda, flour and cinnamon in large bowl. Add shortening and egg. Mix well. Stir in apples until thoroughly incorporated.*

4 *Pour mixture into pan and bake one hour or until cake tests done. Serve hot with sauce.*

Sauce

½ cup sugar	½ cup heavy cream
¼ cup butter	1 tsp. vanilla extract
½ cup brown sugar	

1 *In small saucepan, melt butter; add sugar, brown sugar and vanilla.*

2 *Bring to boil. Remove from heat and add cream.*

3 *Serve over hot cake. Reheats well.*

ROSE ELDER (LEE)

Peach Melba

1 large can peach halves (4)	½ pt. whipped cream (1 can)
1 pt. vanilla ice cream	maraschino cherries, to garnish
4 oz. peach brandy	

1 *In sherbet cups, place 1 peach half; fill with one scoop ice cream.*

2 *Over the ice cream pour one shot glass of peach brandy. Garnish with whipped cream and maraschino cherries.*

3 *Place in freezer about 15 to 20 minutes before serving. Serves 4.*

ROSE ELDER (LEE)

Sweet Potato Pie

1 cup mashed sweet potatoes, cooked
1 cup evaporated milk, undiluted
1 cup light brown sugar, packed
3 eggs, slightly beaten
heavy whipped cream

¼ cup Courvoissier Cognac
1 tsp. cinnamon
1 tsp. nutmeg
¼ tsp. mace
9-inch pie shell, prepared

1 *Preheat oven to 400°.*

2 *Combine sweet potatoes, milk, sugar in a large bowl, mix well. Stir in eggs, cognac, spices and mix well again.*

3 *Pour filling into prepared pie shell, bake about 50 minutes. Cool pie or serve warm with whipped cream on top. Also vanilla ice cream is good. Yields 6-8 servings.*

SHERYL LOTT (LYN)

Cheese Cake

3 large pkgs. cream cheese
1 cup sugar
4 eggs

1 tsp. vanilla
2 small cartons sour cream
1 graham cracker pie crust

1 *Preheat oven to 350°.*

2 *Let cheese soften.*

3 *Mix sugar, eggs and vanilla with cheese. Spoon into crust and bake for 35 or 40 minutes.*

4 *Mix 2 tsp. sugar and ½ tsp. vanilla in each carton of sour cream. Spread on cake and bake 2 minutes at 500°.*

5 *Cool and refrigerate for at least 4 hours. Top with strawberries and serve.*

LEE MORRIS (GREG)

Lee's Instant Trifle Pudding

4-5 boxes Vanilla Instant
   Pudding & Pie Filling
   (Jello Brand, 5½ oz.)
9 tsp. vanilla
18 oz. jar strawberry preserves
1½ pkgs. macaroon cookies,
   crushed
2-3 pound cakes

4-5 pkgs. frozen strawberries,
   thawed (10 oz.)
2 cartons heavy cream
fresh strawberries, refrigerate
   (enough to edge bowl for
   garnish)
1 container Reddi-Whip

These ingredients have been measured for using a clear or plastic circular bowl that measures 14 inches across the top and 4 inches from rim to table.

1 *Prepare vanilla instant pudding in a large bowl according to directions on packages. Add 5 tsp. vanilla to pudding while mixing. Place wax paper on surface of pudding and then place in refrigerator.*

2 *Take thawed strawberries and pour off excess juice. Add 2 tsp. vanilla to strawberries and set aside in a small bowl.*

3 *Cut off edges of pound cake then slice ½ to ¾-inch pieces and fit into clear bowl. Line bowl with cake up to 1½-inch from rim of bowl. (There will be some empty spaces.)*

4 *Spread strawberry preserves over cake in bowl. Allow preserves to fill in openings between cake slices.*

5 *Sprinkle top of preserves with crushed macaroons, sprinkle all over. Place thawed strawberries on top of crushed macaroons.*

6 *Take pudding mixture from refrigerator and pour on top. This should fill in the center all the way to the top of the bowl (1 inch from top).*

7 *Whip heavy cream adding 2 tsp. vanilla until thick and still smooth. Spread on top of pudding. Place in refrigerator.*

8 *When ready to serve, edge the top of trifle with Reddi-Whip making decorative design. Place fresh strawberries on the inside edge of Reddi-Whip for added garnish.*

"You'll be the hit of the community. Your friends will love you and forget all about their diets. It really looks beautiful. When serving just dish out into dessert dishes."

SCOTTY SANDERS (DOUG)

Banana Pudding

¾ cup sugar
2 tbs. flour
¼ tsp. salt
2 cups milk

3 eggs, separated
1 tsp. vanilla
vanilla wafers (approx. ½ box)
6 bananas

1 Preheat oven to 425°.

2 Combine ½ cup sugar, flour, salt in top of double boiler. Stir in milk. Cook over boiling water, stirring constantly until thickened.

3 Cook uncovered for 15 minutes more stirring occasionally. Beat egg yolks. Gradually stir them into hot mixture. Return to double boiler and cook 5 minutes stirring constantly.

4 Place wafers over bottom and side of deep pie pan; slice bananas over wafers.

5 Pour mixture over wafers and banana layer, make another layer of bananas and wafers and pour mixture over again. Repeat with mixture on top.

6 Beat egg whites stiff but not dry in a small bowl. Gradually add remaining ¼ cup sugar and beat until mixture forms stiff peaks. Pile on top of pie and bake for 5 minutes.

JUDY ERSKINE (RANDY)

Freezer Ice Cream Dessert

2 pts. vanilla ice cream
2 sticks butter, melted
1 cup brown sugar

2 cups corn flakes, finely crushed
(may use more or less as
desired)

1 Combine all ingredients except ice cream in bowl and blend well. (Mixture will be dry and sticky.)

2 Layer mixture to bottom and sides of 9-inch square pan (well buttered). Save some for topping.

3 Put 2 to 3 inches of soft (not soupy) ice cream on top of mixture.

4 Cover ice cream with crumb mixture. Cover with foil and freeze. Cut into squares for serving.

IRENE BURNS (GEORGE)

Cheesecake

Crust

1½ cup graham cracker
  crumbs
¼ cup sugar

¼ cup softened butter

1 *Combine all above ingredients in small bowl using fork.*

2 *Press into bottom and sides of spring-lock pan. Set aside.*

(filling)

1 lb. cream cheese (2 pkgs.)
1 lb. Ricotta cheese
1½ cups sugar
4 eggs (added separately)
juice from ½ lemon

3 tbs. corn starch
3 tbs. flour
1 stick butter, melted
1 lb. sour cream

1 *Preheat oven to 350°.*

2 *Mix above ingredients, one at a time in the order listed, in mixing bowl. Add the next one only when the previous are well mixed. Use electric mixer.*

3 *Pour ingredients over crust in pan and bake 1 hour* without opening oven door.

4 *Remove cake and cool 2 hours. Place overnight in refrigerator. Keep cake in pan until just before serving.*

DELLA DICKENSON (GARDNER)

Key Lime Pie

9-inch graham cracker crust
2 8-oz. pkgs. cream cheese
2 cans condensed milk

¾ cup key lime juice
6 egg yolks
whipping cream

1 *In medium size bowl cream the cream cheese.*

2 *Add egg yolks, condensed milk, lime juice and mix well.*

3 *Pour into graham cracker crust. Top with whipped cream and sprinkle with crumbs. Refrigerate.*

JACKIE BAIRD (BUTCH)

Dessert Trifle

1 can strawberries, frozen/
   sweetened
1 small pkg. strawberry jello
1 pound cake

2 pkgs. instant vanilla pudding
1 can whipped cream

1 *Crumble the pound cake. Place it and the strawberries in a bowl and mix together.*

2 *Congeal the jello slightly then mix in pound cake mixture and congeal until set. Top it with vanilla pudding and add whipped cream to taste.*

SHIRLEY LITTLER (GENE)

Pear Crumble

(filling)
6 medium pears
½ cup sugar
1 tsp. lemon peel, grated
3 tbs. lemon juice

(topping)
½ cup whole wheat flour
½ cup white flour
½ cup brown sugar
½ cup white sugar
½ tsp. ginger
½ tsp. cinnamon
¼ tsp. mace
⅓ cup butter (optional)
½ pt. whipping cream,
   flavored with sugar and vanilla
   OR
½ pt. French Vanilla ice cream

1 *Preheat oven to 400°.*

2 *Peel, halve, core, and slice the pears. Toss them lightly with sugar, lemon peel, and juice. Arrange in buttered 9 x 9-inch square pan. Set aside.*

3 *To make topping, combine flour, sugar, ginger, cinnamon and mace in mixing bowl; cut in butter until crumbly. Sprinkle over the pears.*

4 *Bake for 45 minutes or until fruit is tender. Serve warm with whipped cream or ice cream.*

ZXLEMA PRICE

Egg Nog Pie

1 pkg. Knox gelatin, unflavored
¼ tsp. nutmeg
½ cup whipped cream
2 eggs, separated
9-inch pie crust, prepared

1 cup sugar
1 cup sweet milk
¼ tsp. salt
3 tbs. water, cold
2 tbs. rum (whisky, bourbon)

1 *Soak gelatin in cold water. Heat milk.*

2 *In mixing bowl, beat egg yolks with sugar, add salt, and stir hot milk into them.*

3 *Place in double boiler and cook until thickened. Remove from fire. Add gelatin, nutmeg and rum. Then cool.*

4 *Beat with rotary beater, then fold in stiffly beaten egg whites and whipped cream. Pour into pie crust and chill two hours in refrigerator.*

NANCY INMAN (JOE)

Oatmeal Drop Cookies

1⅛ cup honey (or 1¼ cups raw
    sugar)
½ cup oil
2 eggs
6 tbs. unsulphured molasses
1¾ cup whole wheat flour
1 tsp. cinnamon

1 tsp. baking soda
1 tsp. sea salt
2 cups rolled oats
½ cup chopped nuts
1 cup raisins
¾ cup coconut, unsweetened

1 *Preheat oven to 350°.*

2 *Cream honey and oil in mixing bowl until light. Beat in the eggs and then molasses.*

3 *Combine well, flour with the cinnamon, baking soda, and salt and stir into creamed mixture. Then stir in remaining ingredients.*

4 *Drop by teaspoonfuls onto oiled baking sheet. Bake 8 to 10 minutes or until done.*

JUDY ERSKINE (RANDY)

Lemon Refrigerator Cake

¾ cup sugar
6 egg yolks
juice of 2 lemons
whipped cream

1 envelope Knox gelatin
¼ cup water
1 9-inch Angel Food cake
6 egg whites

1 *Mix sugar, egg yolks and lemon juice in sauce pan (or double boiler).*

2 *Cook until mixture thickens slightly, stirring constantly.*

3 *Add gelatin which has been dissolved in ¼ cup water. Cool mixture, but don't chill.*

4 *Beat egg whites with ¾ cup of sugar and add to mixture.*

5 *Break up cake into small pieces (size of small egg) and combine with mixture.*

6 *Put into 9 x 13-inch pan and chill in refrigerator overnight. Serve with whipped cream.*

VERITY CHARLES (BOB)

New Zealand Pavlova

6 egg whites (room
   temperature)
2 tsp. vinegar

2 cups fine sugar
1 tsp. vanilla

1 *Preheat oven to 250°.*

2 *Beat egg whites until frothy but not dry. Pour in sugar slowly while beating. Beat for 10 minutes until very stiff.*

3 *Add vanilla and vinegar. Spread meringue on non-stick paper in the shape of a plate. Bake for 1¼ hours.*

4 *Top with whipped fresh cream and strawberries.*

*" . . . a famous New Zealand dessert called Pavlova which is
simply a large meringue with whipped cream and fresh fruit on top."*

POLLY CRENSHAW (BEN)

Blender Pumpkin Pie

2 envelopes gelatin, unflavored
½ cup cold milk
½ cup milk, boiled
¾ cup firmly packed brown
   sugar
2 cups canned pumpkin
½ tsp. salt

1 tsp. cinnamon
¾ tsp. nutmeg
¼ tsp. ginger
1 cup heavy whipping cream
1 cup ice cubes
9-inch graham cracker crust

1 *Sprinkle gelatin over cold milk in blender. Allow to stand while getting other ingredients.*

2 *Add boiling milk. Cover and process at low speed until gelatin dissolves.*

3 *Add sugar, pumpkin, salt, spices, cream. Cover and process at high speed.*

4 *Add ice cubes one at a time. Process until smooth and ice is melted.*

5 *Chill 5 minutes and then pour into crust. Chill until firm. Add puffs of whipped cream and nutmeg on top of pie.*

SHIRLEY CASPER (BILLY)

Granny's Homemade Ice Cream

2 qts. whole milk
½ cup flour
½ cup cold water
3 cups turbinado sugar*

8 egg yolks, beaten
4 cups heavy cream
2 tsp. vanilla

Turbinado sugar is a partially refined sugar. It may be found in health food stores and some supermarkets.

1 *Pour milk in sauce pan and scald, stirring constantly.*

2 *In the top section of a double boiler, mix a smooth paste of flour and cold water. Continuing to stir, slowly add scalded milk.*

3 *When thickened, cook over hot water about 15 minutes. Add sugar and egg yolks and cook 2 minutes.*

4 *Strain the custard through a fine sieve. Let cool, then add cream and vanilla. Process in an electric or hand-operated ice cream freezer.*

JOAN NIEPORTE (TOM)

Ranger Cookies

½ cup butter, softened
½ cup margarine
1 cup granulated sugar
1 cup brown sugar
2 eggs
2 cups flour, sifted

1 tsp. baking soda
½ tsp. baking powder
½ tsp. salt
1 tbs. vanilla
2 cups quick-cooking oats
2 cups Rice Crispies
1 cup coconut, shredded

1 *Preheat oven to 350°.*

2 *Cream butter, margarine and sugars in mixing bowl. Add eggs and mix well.*

3 *In another bowl, sift together flour, baking soda, baking powder and salt; add to creamed mixture. Add vanilla, oatmeal, cereal and coconut and mix well.*

4 *Form dough into balls about the size of a walnut. Place on a greased cookie sheet and flatten with a fork. Bake in oven 10 to 12 minutes. Yields about 6 dozen.*

LINDA MILLER (JOHNNY)

Lemon Meringue Pie

¾ cup sugar, granulated
¼ tsp. salt
¼ cup flour
4 tbs. cornstarch
2 cups water

1 tbs. butter
¼ cup fresh lemon juice
rind of 1 lemon, grated
9-inch pie shell, baked
3 eggs, separated

1 *Combine sugar, salt, flour and cornstarch in sauce pan and gradually stir in water. Cook, stirring constantly until thickened and smooth.*

2 *Gradually stir in beaten egg yolks to hot mixture. Return to low heat and cook, stirring 2 minutes.*

3 *Stir in butter, lemon juice and rind; cool slightly.*

4 *Pour into baked pie shell and cool.*

5 *Top with a 4 or 5 egg white meringue and brown in oven.*

BARBARA NICKLAUS (JACK)

Jack's Favorite Prune Cake With Sauce

2 cups flour
1½ cups sugar
1 tsp. baking soda
1 tsp. salt
1 tsp. cinnamon
1 tsp. nutmeg
1 cup vegetable oil
½ cup buttermilk
3 eggs

1 cup stewed pitted prunes
1 cup chopped pecans
1 tsp. vanilla

(sauce)
1 cup sugar
½ cup butter
½ cup buttermilk
1 tsp. baking soda

1 *Preheat oven to 350°.*

2 *In mixing bowl, sift together flour, sugar, soda, salt, cinnamon and nutmeg. Add oil, buttermilk and eggs; mix well.*

3 *Stir in prunes, nuts and vanilla.*

4 *Pour into greased and floured baking pan, 13½ x 9 inches. Bake for 35 to 40 minutes or until done.*

5 *When cake is done, make the sauce. Combine all ingredients in a saucepan and bring to a boil, stirring continuously. Pour sauce over each serving of cake.*

MIRIAM BEMAN (DEANE)

Soft Sugar Cookies

1 cup shortening
1½ cups sugar
2 eggs, beaten
¾ cup buttermilk (with ½ tsp.
  soda dissolved in it)

3 cups flour
1 tsp. salt
1 tsp. nutmeg

1 *Preheat oven to 375°.*

2 *In medium size bowl, blend shortening with sugar; add eggs, buttermilk, flour and salt.*

3 *Mix and drop by teaspoonful on greased cookie sheet. Sprinkle with mixture of ¼ cup sugar and nutmeg.*

4 *Bake for about 10 minutes until lightly browned. Cookies are thick in center and cake-like.*

GLORIA DEVLIN (BRUCE)

Pineapple Pavlova

4 egg whites
1 cup sugar, superfine
 granulated
2 tsp. cornstarch
2 tsp. white vinegar
1 tsp. vanilla
1 can (8-oz.) crushed pineapple

3 egg yolks
pulp of 2 passion fruit (2 bananas,
 sliced, may be substituted)
2 tbs. butter
4 tsp. arrowroot
whipped cream

1 *Preheat oven to 250°.*
2 *Line a large baking sheet with waxed paper; grease and dust with cornstarch.*
3 *In mixing bowl, prepare a meringue shell by beating egg whites stiffly, gradually adding sugar as you beat. Fold in cornstarch, vinegar and vanilla.*
4 *Pile into a large circle on the prepared baking sheet, building up the edge of circle to form a shell.*
5 *Bake in oven for 1 hour. Turn off heat and let cool in oven.*
6 *To make the filling, combine pineapple, egg yolks, passion fruit, butter and arrowroot in the top of a double boiler. Bring to a boil, stirring constantly. Remove from heat. Let cool, then chill.*
7 *Pile into shell and garnish with whipped cream.*
   (Note—Crushed strawberries and sliced bananas, added as a garnish, make this dessert even more special.)

SHERRY STANTON (BOB)

Toffee Pie

1 graham cracker crust
10 Heath candy bars, frozen

13 ½ oz. Cool Whip

1 *Place 9 Heath bars in chopper and chop. Mix with Cool Whip and pour into pie crust.*
2 *Sprinkle remaining crumbled Heath bar on top. Keep in freezer until ready to serve. Remove 10 minutes before serving.*

MIRIAM BEMAN (DEANE)

Chocolate Oatmeal Refrigerator Cookies

1 cup flour
½ tsp. salt
½ tsp. soda
½ cup shortening
1 cup brown sugar
1 egg

1 tsp. vanilla
½ tsp. almond extract*
2 1-oz. squares unsweetened
   chocolate, melted and cooled
½ cup walnuts, chopped
1 cup rolled oats, uncooked
   (not instant)

Do not omit the almond extract. It is the secret of the special taste.

1 *Preheat oven to 350°.*

2 *Sift together flour, salt, soda in mixing bowl. Add sugar, shortening, egg, vanilla, almond extract and chocolate. Beat until smooth, about 2 minutes with electric mixer.*

3 *Fold in oats, and then walnuts. Shape in rolls 1½ inches in diameter. Wrap in waxed paper, Saran, or foil and chill thoroughly.*

4 *Slice ½ inch thick. Bake on ungreased cookie sheet for 10-12 minutes. Yields about 5 dozen cookies.*

SUZY MAHAFFEY (JOHN)

Cherry Cream Cheese Pie

(filling)
1 pkg. cream cheese (3 oz.)
½ cup powdered sugar
½ tsp. vanilla
1 cup whipping cream
1 can prepared cherry pie filling

(crust)
1 cup flour, unsifted
2 tbs. powdered sugar
1 stick oleo

1 *Preheat oven to 425°.*

2 *Mix crust ingredients together. Pat into 9-inch buttered pie pan. Bake for 8-10 minutes or until golden brown. Set aside.*

3 *Beat cream cheese, sugar and vanilla together in mixing bowl. Whip cream separately and fold into cheese mixture.*

4 *Pour into cooled pie shell. Chill.*

5 *Spoon cherries on top after filling is firm (adding a few drops of red food coloring to the cherry filling while in the can enhances the appearance).*

JOAN NIEPORTE (TOM)

Carrot Cake

(cake)
1½ cups oil
2 cups sugar
4 eggs, well beaten
3 cups carrots, grated
2 cups cake flour, sifted
½ tsp. salt
2 tsp. soda
2 tsp. cinnamon
2 tsp. all spice

(icing)
½ cup margarine, melted
8 oz. cream cheese
1 box powdered sugar,
    confectionary
½ cup pecans, chopped
½ cup raisins, chopped
½ cup coconut, shredded
1 tsp. vanilla extract

1 *Preheat oven to 325°.*
2 *Cream together oil and sugar, add eggs, carrots, and mix well in medium-size bowl.*
3 *Sift dry ingredients into separate bowl. Then add to carrot mixture a little at a time.*
4 *Beat well and pour into greased 10 x 14-inch cake pan. Bake for 1 hour and cool.*
5 *For icing, combine margarine, cream cheese, and sugar in mixing bowl and beat well.*
6 *Add other ingredients, mixing thoroughly. Spread over cooled cake.*

JOANNE KOHLER (ROY)

Zucchini Cake

3 eggs
1 cup Wesson oil
2 cups sugar
2 cups raw unpeeled zucchini,
    grated
2½ cups flour

1 tsp. baking soda
½ tsp. baking powder
1 tsp. salt
1 cup chopped nuts (walnuts)
2 tsp. vanilla
3 tsp. cinnamon

1 *Preheat oven to 350°.*
2 *Mix together all ingredients in large bowl.*
3 *Pour into 2 floured and greased loaf pans and bake for 1 hour.*

MIRIAM BEMAN (DEANE)

Chocolate Pound Cake

(cake)
½ lb. butter
½ cup shortening
3 cups sugar
5 eggs
1 cup milk
3 cups flour
½ tsp. baking powder
½ tsp. salt
4 tbs. cocoa
1 tbs. vanilla

(glaze)
1 4-oz. bar Baker's German
   Sweet Chocolate
1 tbs. butter
1 egg white
1 cup confectioners sugar
2-3 tsp. water

1 *Preheat oven to 325°.*

2 *In a mixing bowl, cream together butter, shortening, sugar. Add eggs,* one at a time, *blending well after each addition.*

3 *Put flour, baking powder, salt and cocoa into sieve, sift gradually while beating into mixture. Beat about three minutes. Add vanilla.*

4 *Pour into a greased and floured tube cake pan. Bake for 1 hour and 20 minutes. Cool.*

5 *Prepare glaze by first melting chocolate bar and butter in sauce pan.*

6 *In a small bowl, beat egg white until foamy. Gradually add sugar, beating after each addition until smooth.*

7 *Blend in chocolate mix. Add 2 to 3 teaspoons water gradually until you reach desired consistency for glaze. Pour lightly over cooled cake.*

KATHY MENNE (BOB)

Cherry-Cheese Pizza

1 large pie crust (enough to
   cover a pizza tray or a
   regular cookie sheet)
1 can cherry pie filling
8 oz. cream cheese
½ cup sugar

2 eggs
⅓ cup nuts
1 tsp. vanilla
whipped cream

1 *Preheat oven to 350°.*

2 *Roll pie crust dough onto sheet, flute edges, and bake 10-15 minutes. Set aside.*

3 *Blend cream cheese and sugar, then add eggs and beat well. Add chopped nuts and vanilla.*

4 *Pour into partially baked pie crust, then cook 10-15 minutes.*

5 *Spread cherry pie filling over this when it has cooled.*

6 *Finally top with whipped cream, spreading evenly over mixture. Cut and serve. (You may prefer another pie filling.)*

DIANNE CRAWFORD (RICHARD)

English Toffee

1 cup butter
2 cups powdered sugar
2 tsp. cocoa
⅛ tsp. salt
2 eggs
2 tsp. vanilla

1¼-1½ cups vanilla wafers,
   crushed (crush in blender)
1 cup whole pecans
1 tbs. butter
½ pt. whipped cream

1 *Toast pecans in 1 tbs. butter in small fry pan at 350° for 10-15 minutes, stirring occasionally. Set aside.*

2 *Cream the sugar, 1 cup butter, cocoa and salt together in mixing bowl. Beat eggs until light and fluffy, add to mixture. Then add vanilla wafers to mixture. Mix in pecans and vanilla flavoring and mix well.*

3 *Sprinkle bottom of rectangular pyrex dish with vanilla wafer crumbs. Smooth out mixture over crumbs. Sprinkle top with more crumbs. Refrigerate overnight.*

4 *Just before serving, add 2 tbs. powdered sugar and 1 tsp. vanilla to whipped cream, mix together and spread over mixture. Cut into squares and serve.*

SUSAN WIECHERS (JIM)

Napa Valley Wine Cake

(cake)

1 pkg. yellow cake mix
   (18½ oz.)
1 pkg. lemon instant pudding
   mix (4 serving size)
½ cup oil
1 cup dry sherry
4 eggs

(glaze)

1 cup confectioners sugar
2 tbs. fresh lemon juice
   OR
2 tbs. milk

1 *Preheat oven to 350°.*

2 *Blend all ingredients in a large bowl and beat at medium speed for 2 minutes.*

3 *Bake in a greased and floured 10-inch tube pan for 45-55 minutes, until center springs back when lightly touched. Cool right-side up for about 25 minutes, then remove from pan.*

4 *To glaze, blend confectioners sugar with either lemon juice or milk and mix well. Drizzle over cake.*

DIANNE CRAWFORD (RICHARD)

Strawberry-Banana Mold

1 large pkg. strawberry jello
1 pkg. frozen strawberries (use
   2 for large salad)
2 large bananas

1 can crushed pineapple (large or
   small depending on size of
   salad)
1 cup boiled water
1 cup sour cream

1 *Dissolve jello in water. Add frozen strawberries, banana slices and pineapple and stir until strawberries are thawed.*

2 *Congeal half of this mixture in a pan and set the rest aside.*

3 *When congealed, spread surface with sour cream then pour on rest of jello and congeal again.*

MRS. POLLARD (SUSAN WIECHER'S MOTHER)

Booze Cake

(cake)
½ cup butter
1 cup white sugar
3 eggs, separated
⅓ cup brandy
2 cups all-purpose flour
2 tsp. baking powder
½ tsp. baking soda
pinch salt
1 tsp. cinnamon
1 tsp. cloves, ground
1 tsp. nutmeg
½ cup chocolate (instant mix)
1 cup raisins
1 cup walnuts, chopped

(icing)
½ cup butter
2 cups powdered sugar, sifted
1 egg, beaten
2 tbs. brandy

1 Preheat oven to 350°.

2 Boil raisins with 3 cups of water in a sauce pan for 20 minutes; strain and save ½ cup of the liquid. Cool.

3 Cream butter and sugar gradually, add beaten egg yolks, then raisin water and brandy.

4 Sift flour 3 times with baking powder, soda, salt, spices and chocolate. Add to butter mixture and stir until well mixed.

5 Add walnuts and raisins; fold in stiffly beaten egg whites.

6 Pour into two 8-inch layer pans (greased and lined with waxed paper). Bake for 30 to 35 minutes or until done. Cool.

7 To make icing, in a separate bowl cream butter until real soft and fluffy. Add sugar gradually, beating well after each addition.

8 Then add egg and brandy. Beat until real fluffy. Put on cooled cake.

IRENE REAVES (CALVIN)

Wine Cake

¾ cup cream sherry
¾ cup oil
1 box yellow cake mix
1 box instant Jello Pudding,
    vanilla
4 eggs, slightly beaten

1 tsp. nutmeg
⅓ cup confectionary sugar
2 tbs. butter, melted
pinch salt
2 tbs. wine, warmed

1 *Preheat oven to 350°.*

2 *Combine cake mix, jello pudding and nutmeg in mixing bowl.*

3 *Mix wine and oil together in separate bowl.*

4 *Add oil-wine mixture to dry ingredients. Stir until smooth. Do not over mix.*

5 *Fold in slightly beaten eggs. Pour into well greased and floured cake pan. Bake approximately one hour. Test for doneness at about 45 minutes.*

6 *Sift confectionary sugar into bowl. Add butter, salt and wine and mix thoroughly. Dribble over cake for icing.*

KATHY MENNE (BOB)

Cathedral Windows

6 oz. chocolate chips
4 tbs. butter
2 eggs, slightly beaten
1 cup vanilla wafers, crushed

1 cup nuts, chopped
1 cup confectionary sugar
1 pkg. miniature marshmallows,
    colored
1 pkg. flaky cocoanut

1 *Melt butter and chocolate chips together in sauce pan and set aside until warm.*

2 *Put mixture in bowl and add all other ingredients except coconut.*

3 *Separate mixture into 4 parts. Roll each section out log style in the coconut. Wrap in foil and refrigerate, or freeze. Slice and serve as a candy type snack.*

**"Surprisingly, it isn't that sweet, despite
the ingredients. Very attractive for the
holidays, but mustn't be left around as it
will get sticky if it gets warm."**

LEE MORRIS (GREG)

Lee's Sweet Potato Pie

2 lbs. yams	¾ cup sugar
1 stick butter	¼ cup brown sugar
1 tsp. cinnamon	2 large eggs
1 tsp. salt	½ cup heavy cream
¼ tsp. mace	½ cup evaporated milk
¼ tsp. ginger	½ cup rum (optional – if not
¼ tsp. cardamom	used add more milk)
2 tsp. orange or lemon peel	2 9-inch pie crusts, unbaked

1 *Preheat oven to 350°.*

2 *Cook yams in skin in pot with water to cover. Boil until fork tender (very tender). Peel while hot and weigh enough for 2 lbs. (3 medium yams).*

3 *Place yams in large mixing bowl. Add stick of butter and blend with mixer at lowest speed.*

4 *Continue mixing while adding the remaining ingredients in order listed. Mix until very smooth. Do not shake beaters when removing.*

5 *Pour mixture into two pie crusts (evenly). Top with some cinnamon and nutmeg.*

6 *Bake for 45 minutes to 1 hour.*

RACHEL WADKINS (LANNY)

Chocolate Indians (Brownies)

2 eggs	½ cup pecans, chopped
1 cup sugar	1 tsp. vanilla
½ cup cocoa	½ cup melted butter (1 stick)
½ cup flour	dash of cinnamon

1 *Preheat oven to 325°.*

2 *Beat eggs, sugar, and butter together in mixing bowl. Sift in flour with cocoa and mix well. Then add nuts, vanilla, and cinnamon.*

3 *Bake 20 to 30 minutes in a 9 x 9-inch greased and floured pan. Cut into squares and lightly sprinkle with powdered sugar.*

CAROL REASOR (MIKE)

Deep-Dish Blackberry Pie

1 cup sugar	1 cup flour
⅓ cup flour	½ tsp. salt
1 tsp. lemon peel, grated	⅓ cup plus 1 tbs. shortening
8 cups fresh or frozen	2-3 tbs. cold water
blackberries, slightly thawed	
1 tbs. butter or margarine	

1 *Preheat oven to 425°.*

2 *Mix sugar, ⅓ cup flour and lemon peel together in bowl; toss with fruit and then turn into ungreased baking dish 8 x 8 x 2 inches and dot with butter.*

3 *Mix 1 cup flour and salt into separate bowl. Blend in shortening thoroughly. Sprinkle in water, 1 tbs. at a time, mixing until flour is moistened and pastry almost cleans side of bowl. Gather pastry into ball.*

4 *Roll into a 9-inch square on lightly floured surface. Fold pastry in half, cut slits near center. Unfold over fruit in baking dish; fold pastry edges under (do not attempt to seal dish).*

5 *Bake until crust is brown and filling bubbles through slits, 40-45 minutes. Serve with vanilla ice cream while pie is still hot.*

CINDY CURL (ROD)

Blackberry Pie

2 cups plain flour	2 pkgs. frozen blackberries, thawed
⅔ cups shortening	1 cup sugar
¾ tsp. salt	2 to 3 tbs. tapioca
water, as needed	pinch salt

1 *Sift flour and salt. Cut in shortening with a knife. Add water as needed to mold into two balls (do not knead dough). Roll out and place in pie dish. Trim off excess dough.*

2 *Place blackberries in uncooked pie crust. Sprinkle sugar, tapioca and salt over top of berries. Place a few slices of butter over berries and put on top crust. Trim again. Poke holes in top crust with fork.*

3 *Bake at 400° for 15 minutes. Reduce heat to 350° and cook 45 minutes longer or until golden brown. Serve when cooled with ice cream.*

SANDY FLECKMAN (MARTY)

Hello Dolly Brownies

2½ cups graham cracker
  crumbs
1 tsp. cinnamon
¼ lb. butter, melted
1 can condensed milk

1 large pkg. chocolate chips
1 cup chopped pecans
1 cup coconut
1 tsp. vanilla

1 *Preheat oven to 325°.*

2 *Mix crumbs, cinnamon and butter together in medium-size bowl. Spread all but ½ cup of mixture on bottom of greased 9 x 12-inch pan.*

3 *Mix the rest of the ingredients together and smooth over crumb mixture in pan.*

4 *Sprinkle reserve crumbs on top and bake for 35 minutes. Let cool and cut into squares.*

VIVIENNE PLAYER (GARY)

Carrot Cake

1½ cups oil
2 cups sugar
4 eggs, well beaten
3 cups grated carrots

2 cups sifted cake flour
½ tsp. salt
2 tsp. cinnamon
2 tsp. allspice
2 tsp. soda

1 *Cream oil and sugar together, add eggs and carrots.*

2 *Sift all dry ingredients to carrot mixture a little at a time, mixing well.*

3 *Pour into greased baking pan, 10 x 14 inches.*

4 *Bake at 325° for 1 hour; cool and add icing.*

Icing

½ cup margarine, melted
8 oz. cream cheese
1 box powdered sugar

½ cup pecans, chopped
½ cup raisins, chopped
½ cup coconut
1 tsp. vanilla extract

1 *In mixing bowl cream all ingredients well; spread on cooled cake.*

DORA HEAD
(Rose Elder's Grandmother)

Grandma's Chocolate Roll

5 egg yolks
5 egg whites
1 cup powdered sugar
3 tbs. cocoa
2 squares chocolate

⅛ tsp. cream of tartar
1 tsp. vanilla extract
1 tbs. butter
2 tbs. white syrup
1 pt. whipping cream

Cake Roll

1 *Mix well: egg yolks, sugar and cocoa. Beat egg whites until stiff; fold into mixture.*

2 *Pour onto lightly greased-floured cookie sheet (9 x 12-inch). Bake at 325° until done, about 18-20 minutes. Be sure to watch attentively.*

3 *Place on large platter or cutting board to roll the cake.*

4 *Mix whipping cream until stiff. Pour onto cake. Carefully roll (overlapping face down), and place in refrigerator.*

Chocolate Syrup

1 *Melt chocolate in double boiler. Add butter, vanilla, cream of tartar and syrup.*

2 *Cook until smooth, stirring often. Do not overcook.*

3 *Just before serving, pour chocolate syrup over entire cake roll. (Hershey's canned chocolate syrup may be substituted, if you do not wish to make your own.) Slice into desired pieces. Yields 8 servings.*

HINTS: Add chocolate syrup to individual servings if entire portion is not used at one setting. Delicious served over squares of vanilla ice cream.

NOTES

V

Fish & Seafood

Editor's Note

FISH AND SEAFOOD

As my brother Sonny says, the best way to prepare a fish dish is with fresh fish. It is a very delicate food and should be seasoned with gentle restraint. Some favorite seasonings that blend well are wine, lemon, butter, chives, parsley and cream. Sonny says if you have fresh fish and want to freeze them, do not clean until you are ready to cook. This helps preserve the flavor. (He's a fisherman, not me.)

SHERRY STANTON (BOB)

Biloxi Seafood Gumbo

1 lb. raw shrimp, peeled &
  de-veined
1 lb. fresh crabmeat
1 can each tomatoes and
  okra
2 onions, chopped
4 cloves garlic, finely minced
4 stalks celery, finely chopped
3 tbs. cooking oil

1 cup parsley, chopped
2 green peppers, chopped
½ lb. ham, diced
2 strips bacon, cut up
2 slices bologna, chopped
½ lb. pork sausage
6 cups water

1 *In heavy pot, fry okra and tomatoes, bologna, sausage, and bacon in oil until very brown and until liquids evaporate.*

2 *Add remaining ingredients except shrimp and crabmeat. Add water and simmer one hour.*

3 *Twenty minutes before serving, add shrimp and crabmeat, simmer. Add salt and pepper to taste. Serve over rice in a soup bowl.*

"This recipe is a local dish from the Biloxi area that Bob loves. I hope that it will add a variety to the cookbook. Try it, you'll like it."

MILLIE HARRIS

Fish and Eggs Dish

1 small can pink salmon
½ stick margarine
1 cup cooked grits or rice
4 eggs

¼ tsp. Season All
¼ tsp. white pepper
¼ tsp. garlic powder or salt

1 *Cook rice or grits according to direction on box.*

2 *Saute salmon in margarine slowly until very hot. (If salmon is drying, add more margarine).*

3 *Beat eggs in mixing bowl. Add Season All, pepper and garlic.*

4 *Lightly fold beaten egg mixture into salmon in skillet like an omelet (heat should be even tempered with skillet hot enough to cook eggs). Serve immediately over rice or grits. Yields 4 servings.*

MARYROSE POTT (JOHNNY)

Courtbouillon

1 cup bacon drippings	1 bunch green onions, chopped
2 large onions, chopped	2 tbs. parsley
1 green pepper, chopped	¼ tsp. basil
4 stalks celery, chopped	¼ tsp. oregano
1 cup good red wine	1 large can tomato sauce
4 dashes Tabasco	salt to taste
¼ cup Worcestershire Sauce	2 lbs. fresh fish (lemon fish,
2 bay leaves	snapper, red fish, black fish),
	thoroughly boned, and cubed

1 *Saute all vegetables in bacon drippings until transparent. Add other ingredients and cook slowly 3-4 hours. Add water if needed. (A heavy pot is best to use.)*

2 *About 25 minutes before serving, add cubes of fish, and increase heat. Cook for about 20 minutes.*

3 *Serve over rice with hot french bread and tossed salad.*

Alternate: Half bake a fish (30 minutes at 350°), then add sauce on top and cook in oven for 30 minutes.

LINDA MILLER (JOHNNY)

Bass in Beer Batter

5 fresh bass fillets	⅔ cup beer
1 egg	1 cup flour
salt and pepper to taste	

1 *Beat egg slightly, add beer and flour. Mix lightly until batter is smooth.*

2 *Dip bass fillets in batter and fry in hot oil (about 340°) until done; approximately 5 minutes on each side, depending on thickness of fillets. Serve fish with fresh lemon or soy sauce.*

**"Serve with fresh corn on the cob, home grown
sliced tomatoes with vinegar, and warm bread. For dessert,
icy watermelon or lemon meringue pie."**

CAROLE BREWER (GAY)

Tuna Salad

2 cans tuna, regular size
1 box frozen green peas,
   thawed
2 small bottles cocktail onions,
   sliced
1 tbs. curry powder
2 tbs. soy sauce

1½ cups celery, chopped
1 can crisp Chinese noodles*
1 cup mayonnaise
1 tbs. lemon juice

Just before serving, mix noodles into salad to ensure crispness.

1 *Mix mayonnaise, lemon juice, curry powder, and soy sauce together.*

2 *In large mixing bowl, put tuna, green peas, onions and celery. Pour mayonnaise dressing over tuna mixture and blend well.*

**"Serve with sourdough bread and
Pouilly-Fuisse Wine."**

BRENDA DENT (JIM)

Salmon Croquettes

1 lb. can salmon
¼ cup bell pepper, chopped
¼ cup onion, chopped or
   minced
¼ cup celery, chopped
   (or ¼ tsp. celery seed)
1 tsp. Worcestershire sauce
1 tsp. soy sauce

½ cup flour
1 tsp. baking powder
⅛ tsp. thyme
⅛ tsp. oregano
1 cup vegetable oil
½ cup coating mix or meal

1 *Drain salmon, place in mixing bowl and crush large chunks. Add flour and baking powder, then remaining ingredients except oil. Mix thoroughly.*

2 *Spoon out salmon mixture according to preferred size and flatten into patties. Sprinkle with coating mix or meal on both sides. Fry in hot oil to desired crispness or browness. Serve with grits or home fries for breakfast or with a green salad for lunch and dinner.*

BETTY FORD (GERALD R. FORD)

Prawn Madras Curry

1 tbs. coriander
1 tsp. turmeric
½ tsp. dry mustard
½ tsp. ginger
½ tsp. cumin
½ tsp. coarse red chile pepper
grated coconut

lemon juice, tamarind juice or
    vinegar
2 cloves garlic, minced
1 small onion, chopped
ghee or butter
12 to 18 shelled cooked prawns or
    large shrimp
1 tbs. thick coconut milk*

Coconut Milk—If fresh coconuts are handy, the milk can be made as follows: crack open the coconut and remove the dark outer skin. Cut the white meat into small pieces. Put in a blender with a little water and whirl until finely chopped. One good-sized coconut yields about 3 cups grated meat. Wrap 3 cups of the chopped or grated coconut in cheesecloth and place in a strainer over a large, deep bowl. Pour 1 quart hot water over the wrapped coconut. Let drain 10 minutes; then, into another bowl, squeeze out milk through the cheesecloth.

Canned coconut contains sugar, so if used in place of fresh, the sweetness must be taken into account lest it change the flavor of the dish. To make an acceptable milk from canned coconut, combined 2 cans coconut with 1½ cups whole milk. Gradually bring to a boil, then remove from heat and let stand until cool. Strain through at least two layers of cheesecloth, squeezing out the liquid.

1 *Blend the first 6 ingredients with just enough lemon juice to make a paste. Let this curry paste set to develop all the flavors while you prepare the prawn mixture. (The composition of the paste may be varied to taste by using minced fresh chiles instead of dried, or by using a flavored vinegar.)*

2 *Saute garlic and onion 3 minutes in a little ghee (preferably) or butter. Add the curry paste and simmer gently over low heat for 4 to 5 minutes. Add prawns and coconut milk. Continue to cook, stirring lightly, just until seafood is warmed through and liquid is absorbed. Sprinkle with grated coconut and serve with rice. Serves 4 to 6.*

ROSE ELDER (LEE)

Shrimp and Rice in Wine

2 lbs. shrimp
⅓ cup lemon juice
2 cloves garlic, finely chopped
½ cup butter
1 cup almonds, chopped or
    slivered

½ cup dry white wine
dash of Tabasco
4 cups cooked rice*
½ cup olive oil

Cook rice with ½ cup chopped chives, ½ tsp. saffron, 1 tsp. chicken bouillon.

1 Shell shrimp and remove veins.
2 Slice in half. Add mixture of olive oil and lemon juice. Let stand 2 hours, turning shrimp once.
3 Drain, reserving liquid.
4 Saute shrimp and garlic in butter until shrimp turn pink.
5 Remove garlic from pan and place shrimp on hot platter.
6 Add almonds to pan in which shrimp were cooked. Add reserved olive oil and lemon juice liquid, dash tobasco and white wine.
7 Heat and pour over shrimp. Serve over rice. Yields 6-8 servings.

Quick hint: If shrimp are frozen they shell and de-vein easily when half-thawed. You will find them easy to clean and slice in half.

JANE SIMS (SAM)

Shrimp Louisville

¼ cup butter
1 cup bread crumbs
1 clove garlic, finely
chopped
4 tbs. parsley, chopped
3½ cups canned tomatoes
¼ cup flour

½ cup heavy cream
2 tbs. Worcestershire Sauce
½ cup sherry
dash of Angustora Bitters
(optional)
shrimp or lobster
(as much as you like)
salt and pepper, to taste

1 *Saute garlic in butter until slightly brown. Add parsey and 3 cups tomatoes. Cook 5 minutes.*

2 *In separate dish, mix flour with remaining ½ cup tomatoes forming smooth paste. Add to tomatoes, garlic and parsley and cook 2 minutes longer.*

3 *Add cream, Worcestershire Sauce, sherry and bitters. Cook 5 minutes and then add cleaned and deveined shrimp or lobster.*

4 *Pour into 2 qt. casserole dish. Cover with bread crumbs and dot with butter. Bake in 375° oven for 20 minutes. Serve with white rice.*

"It's delicious!"

IRENE REAVES (CALVIN)

Gourmet Shrimp

2 lbs. fresh shrimp
(or 2 pkgs. thawed quick-
frozen shrimp)
4 tbs. butter or margarine

1 clove garlic, minced
¾ tsp. salt
¼ cup chopped parsley

1 *Wash shrimp in strainer under cold water, remove shells and devein. Place in bowl, cover chilled until ready to use.*

2 *Just before serving time, melt butter in medium sized skillet and add parsley, garlic and salt. Saute 1 minute. Add shrimp and saute, stirring often (2 to 4 minutes or just until shrimp are firm and pink). Time carefully, overcooking makes shrimp tough. Serve immediately. Yields 8 servings.*

**"Shrimp can be prepared ahead of time,
ready for last minute sauteing."**

VIRGINIA IVERSON (DON)
Shrimp and Crab Casserole

1 pt. mayonnaise	1 can water chestnuts, diced
1 16 oz. can crab	2 hard boiled eggs, cut up
1½ lb. cooked shrimp	½ lb. mushrooms, sliced
2 cups diced celery	½ cup sliced almonds
1 green pepper, chopped	1 cup bread crumbs
1 medium onion, chopped	½ stick butter

1 *Mix mayonnaise, crab, shrimp, celery, green pepper, onions, water chestnuts, eggs, mushrooms, and almonds in casserole dish.*

2 *In sauce pan, melt butter. Add bread crumbs and mix well.*

3 *Cover casserole mixture with butter bread crumbs and bake uncovered at 350° for 40 minutes.*

ROSE ELDER (LEE)
Seafood Stuffed Green Peppers

5 medium size green peppers	¾ cup mayonnaise
½ lb. shrimp, peeled and de-veined	1 tsp. curry powder
	½ tsp. salt
1 6-oz. pkg. frozen crabmeat, thawed & drained	2 tbs. capers
	dash of Season All
1½ cup rice, cooked	½ cup bread crumbs
½ cup celery, chopped	⅓ cup butter or margarine
½ cup onion, chopped	
2 tbs. pimento, chopped	

1 *Cut top of each pepper and remove seeds and membrane. Cook in boiling salted water for 5 minutes. Drain well and set aside.*

2 *Combine shrimp, crabmeat, rice, celery, onion and pimento. In separate bowl, combine mayonnaise, curry powder, salt and pepper. Stir into crab-meat mixture, mixing thoroughly.*

3 *Stuff peppers with seafood mixture. Sprinkle each with bread crumbs and dot with butter.*

4 *Place stuffed peppers in deep baking dish filled with ½ inch hot water.*

5 *Bake at 350° for 30 minutes. Yields 5 servings.*

MIRIAM BEMAN (DEANE)

Fish-Cheese Roll-Ups

1 pkg. fresh or frozen fish
    fillets
2 to 3 very thin slices swiss
    cheese
3 tbs. onion, chopped
¼ tsp. fresh ground black
    pepper
½ tsp. parsley

1 egg, beaten
¼ cup butter or margarine
⅔ cup fine dry bread crumbs
½ tsp. salt
1 tsp. prepared mustard

1 *If fish is frozen, allow to thaw in refrigerator.*
2 *Cut fillets into strips 1¼ inches wide and 6-8 inches long.*
3 *Cut cheese into 1-inch wide strips and trim one strip to fit each fillet strip.*
4 *Combine parsley, onion, mustard, bread crumbs (3 tbs.), salt and pepper and spread 1 tablespoon on each fillet-cheese strip.*
5 *Roll up like jelly roll and skewer with toothpick.*
6 *Dip whole roll in beaten egg and then into bread crumbs (remaining).*
7 *Heat butter in skillet. Add fillet rolls and fry over moderate heat, turning to brown on all sides, for about 6 minutes. Serve 3 or 4 to a portion. Yields 3 or 4 servings.*

PEARL GREEN (ALBERT)

Broiled Stuffed Flounder

3 to 4 lbs. whole flounder
(with center bone removed)
¼ cup lemon juice
3 tbs. margarine, melted
1 tsp. lemon-pepper seasoning
½ tsp. Old Bay Seafood
Seasoning
¼ tsp. paprika

1 lb. backfin crabmeat
1 tbs. onion, finely chopped
1 tsp. parsley flakes
¼ cup bread crumbs
½ cup heavy cream
salt and pepper, to taste

1 *Mix lemon juice, margarine, lemon-pepper and Old Bay seasoning together and brush over fish, inside and outside. Let marinate while stuffing is being prepared.*

2 *Mix crabmeat, onions, parsley, bread crumbs, cream, salt and pepper in small dish.*

3 *Place crabmeat mixture inside fish and secure open side with toothpick or skewers.*

4 *Baste again with marinating liquid and sprinkle lightly with paprika.*

5 *Broil 4 to 6 inches away from fire for approximately 5 to 8 minutes on each side. Serve with baked potato, tossed salad, and a favorite beverage.*

"In our home we are all 'lovers of the links' because we are involved. The task of menu-planning has to be balanced as well as appetizing, and often prepared in a hurry. There are times, however, when I feel the meal deserves a little special touch. Here is one that brings the 'yummies to the tummies' and is one of Al's favorites."

SIS GOEKEN (DICK)

Trout Marguery

1 *Clean and fillet one large trout. Cover the heads, bones, tail in a saucepan with 1 qt. water. Add the following:*

1 sliced onion	**1-2 cloves garlic**
4 sprigs parsley	**2 tsp. salt**
2 bay leaves	**¼ tsp. red pepper**
6-7 whole cloves	

2 *Boil until stock has evaporated to approximately 1 pint of stock. While this boils, make the following sauce in a double boiler:*

2 tbs. butter	**1 tsp. salt**
2 tbs. flour	**1 cup milk**

When thick, turn out fire. Reheat later.

3 *Place fillets in a baking dish; salt and pepper them. Pour 1½ cups of fish stock over them. Cover dish with foil. Bake 20 minutes at 300°.*

4 *To the white sauce, add 4 beaten egg yolks. Cook slowly. Add the following and beat with a whisk:*

½ cup fish stock	**1 tbs. lemon juice**
4 tbs. sherry	**½ cup mushrooms, canned**
¼ lb. melted butter	**2 doz. shrimp that have been boiled**

5 *Remove fillets from oven. Remove from baking dish carefully and place on hot platter. Pour sauce over the fish and serve immediately. Garnish as desired.*

NANCY INMAN (JOE)

Shrimp and Artichoke Casserole

6 tbs. butter
5 tbs. unbleached white flour
¾ cup milk
¾ cup heavy cream
salt and pepper, to taste
¼ cup Parmesan cheese, grated

1 #2 can artichoke hearts, drained
1 lb. cooked shrimp
¼ lb. fresh mushrooms, sliced
¼ cup sherry
1 tbs. Worcestershire Sauce
paprika

1 *Preheat oven to 375°.*

2 *Melt butter and saute mushrooms for 2 minutes. Stir in flour and blend. Gradually add milk and cream, stirring constantly. When thickened, add salt and pepper.*

3 *Arrange artichokes on bottom of baking dish and place shrimp over them.*

4 *Add sherry and Worcestershire to mushroom sauce and pour over dish.*

5 *Sprinkle with cheese and paprika. Bake 30 minutes. Serve over rice. Yields 4 large servings.*

"Serve with tossed salad. In salad include fresh mushrooms, broccoli flowers, sliced zucchini, tomatoes, carrots, celery, onions, Romaine lettuce and Boston lettuce."

CAROL REASOR (MIKE)

Charocal Broiled Salmon

3-4 lb. salmon fillet

Marinade

2-3 tbs. cooking oil
½ cup butter
2-3 tbs. fresh lemon juice
garlic salt (to taste)

salt and pepper (to taste)
Johnny Dock's Seasoning Salt
** (to taste)**
paprika

1 *Make marinade and set aside.*
2 *Heat coals until they reach their peak in heat.*
3 *Place salmon, flesh side down, over heat for 3-4 minutes. Turn over so that skin side is down.*
4 *Make a tent of tin foil, baste with marinade.*
   TIPS: Spices must be put in to taste. Start with ¼ tsp. of each and add what is needed. The most important thing to remember when barbecuing salmon is NOT TO OVERCOOK.

"We like to start with freshly caught salmon, second best is purchased at our local fish market during salmon season. If all else fails, use fresh-frozen. Since our favorite way is cooked over the charcoal coals, this is the recipe I have used."

KATHEE McCORD (GARY)

Paella

2 lbs. chicken breasts and thighs (cubed)
1 lb. lobster chunks
1 lb. scallops
½ lb. shrimp
1 lb. frozen peas
8 clams (optional)
8 cooked artichoke hearts (optional)
2 cups rice, uncooked
5 cups chicken stock
3 cups canned tomatoes
½ cup instant chopped onion
1 tbs. salt
1 tsp. oregano
⅓ cup water
½ tsp. pepper
1 tsp. saffron
¼ cup oil

1 *Rub chicken and seafood with mixture of salt, oregano and pepper. Brown in oil and set aside.*

2 *Soften onion in water, combine saffron and chicken stock and bring to boil.*

3 *Combine onion, stock, tomatoes, peas and rice in casserole or paella pan.*

4 *Arrange chicken and fish over top. Cover and bake at 325° for one hour.*

5 *Add shrimp and clams. Cover and bake 20 minutes longer (until clams steam open). Garnish with artichoke hearts. Yields 8-10 servings.*

NOTES

VI

Meats & Entrees

Editor's Note

MEATS

One of the most important culinary skills is learning how to handle meat. There is an art in turning the least costly cuts into magnificent dishes (I learned this in Italy and France this winter). Stewing meats are often overcooked. They are much better when carefully cooked and properly seasoned. Your more expensive cuts should be prepared with the best of care also, minding never to overcook or cook too fast. When meats are seasoned and cooked properly they are excellent complemented in their own juices. When there are juices left, they are very good to flavor your vegetables.

JILLEAN WILLIAMS (JOE)

Beef Stroganoff

6 tbs. butter
1 cup onion, finely chopped
1 garlic clove
2 tbs. tomato paste
2 tbs. flour
1 cup beef bouillon
   (the canned soup type)
1 lb. fresh mushrooms, sliced

¼ cup sour cream
½ cup heavy cream
1 tsp. Worcestershire sauce
½ tsp. salt
Pinch ground pepper
Fresh dill or parsley
   (optional – only for garnish)
2 lbs. fillet of beef

Early in the day

1 *Melt 4 tbs. butter in heavy skillet. Add onion and garlic. Saute until golden and tender.*

2 *Add tomato paste and mix well. Add flour and blend. Gradually add beef bouillon. Stir while cooking over medium heat until smooth and thick. Add mushrooms, simmer 10 minutes.*

3 *Refrigerate this mixture until half an hour before serving.*

4 *To prepare the beef fillet for cooking, trim fat and cut meat crosswise into ½ inch slices. Cut the slices across the grain into ½ inch strips. Cover and refrigerate.*

5 Half an hour before serving *place the sauce mixture on low flame to heat gently. Melt 2 tbs. butter in large skillet. Add beef strips to cover bottom of the pan. Sear quickly, and remove meat immediately the outside has browned. Add more until all the meat is seared but pink on the inside.*

6 *To the sauce mixture, add sour cream, heavy cream, Worcestershire sauce, salt and pepper, and stir well. Allow to simmer and add the beef strips for a few minutes until they heat through. Do not allow the mixture to boil or the cream will curdle. Garnish with the dill or parsley.*

"Serve with noodles or rice — we prefer rice. Of course, all the above can be done at the same time, but there is sometimes an advantage in being able to prepare some of it ahead of time."

VINCENT E. REED
(Supt. D.C. Public Schools)

Beef Stroganoff

3 tbs. flour	2 tsp. Worcestershire sauce
1½ tsp. salt	¼ cup water
¼ tsp. pepper	1 can (10½ oz.) can cream of
1 lb. beef tenderloin or	chicken or mushroom soup,
sirloin ¼ inch thick, cut in	undiluted
¼ inch strips	1 cup mushrooms, sliced &
1 clove garlic, chopped	drained
¼ cup butter or margarine	¼ cup commercial sour cream
½ cup onion, chopped	2 tbs. dry sherry, or to taste

1 *Combine flour, salt, pepper. Trim fat from meat and rub meat with garlic. Coat with flour mixture.*

2 *Heat butter in hot Dutch oven; brown meat strips, turning them often. Add onion and saute until golden. Add water, stirring to dissolve brown residue in bottom of Dutch oven. Add soup, mushrooms, Worcestershire sauce, and cook uncovered, over low heat, stirring occasionally until mixture is thick and meat is fork tender—about 20 minutes.*

3 *Just before serving, stir in sour cream and wine. Cook slowly until heated thoroughly. Do not boil. Serve with hot, fluffy rice or wild rice, boiled noodles or mashed potatoes. Serves 4 or 5.*

ALMA GENUS (LLOYD)

Chitterlings

10 lbs. chitterlings	½ tsp. Accent
2 cups burgundy or sauterne	beer
wine	salt & pepper, to taste
⅛ tsp. garlic powder	bayleaf

1 *Clean and wash chitterlings thoroughly.*

2 *Pour off all water. Cover with beer. Add wine, garlic powder, bayleaf, Accent, salt and pepper.*

3 *Bring to a boil. Lower heat and simmer until done (approx. 4 hours). Serve with potato salad, leaf greens and cornbread. Serves 4-6 people.*

PATRICIA SPAULDING (AARON)

Baked Pork Chops

6 medium-sized pork chops
2 eggs
2 tbs. milk

1 cup crumbled saltine crackers
3 tbs. vegetable oil
salt and pepper, to taste

1 *Salt and pepper pork chops to taste.*

2 *In shallow dish, beat eggs and milk.*

3 *Dip pork chops in egg mixture and then in crumbled saltines.*

4 *Brown pork chops on both sides in vegetable oil in heavy skillet. (Do not cook pork chops. They should remain in skillet only long enough to lightly brown cracker coating).*

5 *Remove browned pork chops from skillet and wrap each separately in aluminum foil.*

6 *Bake in oven at 325° for 40 minutes.*

JUDY ERSKINE (RANDY)

Cheese-Beef Noodle Casserole

½ lb. ground beef
1 onion, chopped
1 pkg. fine noodles (8 oz.),
    cooked and drained
2½ cups cheddar cheese,
    shredded

1 can (15-oz.) tomato sauce
½ tsp. salt
pepper, to taste
grated Parmesan cheese (optional)

1 *In skillet, saute beef and onions until beef is lightly browned and onions are tender.*

2 *Combine with noodles, sauce, 1 cup cheddar cheese, salt, pepper and pour into greased 12 x 8 x 2-inch casserole dish.*

3 *Top with remaining 1½ cups of cheddar cheese. Sprinkle with Parmesan. Bake in oven at 350° for 30 minutes or until top is golden brown. Yields 4-6 servings.*

DIANE ZIOBRO (BILLY)

Beef Stroganoff

2 lbs. beef tenderloin or
   sirloin steak
¼ cup butter
½ lb. fresh mushrooms, sliced
2 cans (10-oz.) condensed
   beef broth
½ cup onions, chopped

¼ cup catsup
1½ tsp. garlic salt
⅓ cup flour
2 cups sour cream
8 to 10 ozs. noodles
3 tbs. butter

1 *Cut meat across the grain into ¾-inch slices, then into strips 3 x ½ inches. Set aside.*

2 *Melt butter in large skillet. Cook and stir sliced mushrooms in butter. Remove mushrooms.*

3 *In same skillet, brown meat. When meat is brown, stir in broth, reserving ⅔ cup. Stir in onion, catsup and garlic salt. Cover and simmer 15 minutes.*

4 *Blend reserved broth and flour. Stir into meat. Add mushrooms, heat to boiling; stirring constantly. Boil and stir one minute. Then stir in sour cream. Heat thoroughly.*

5 *Cook noodles as directed on package. Drain. Toss with 3 tablespoons butter. Serve with stroganoff. Yields 6 to 8 servings. Serve with a vegetable of your choice and dinner rolls.*

ROSE ELDER (LEE)

Short Ribs of Beef, Easy

4 lean short ribs
1 pkg. Lipton's onion soup

1 cooking bag

1 *Wash ribs with cold water and pat lightly with paper towel.*

2 *Place in cooking bag. Pour in onion soup, shake to make sure all sides are covered, seal bag well.*

3 *Place in shallow baking pan, punch about 8 holes in bag with fork. Cook in preheated oven at 350° for about 1½ hours, or until cooked to your taste.*

4 *Remove from bag. Place on hot platter. Serve hot. Yields 3 servings.*

JACKIE BAIRD (BUTCH)

Cottage Pie

3 lbs. ground beef
2 large onions, sliced
2 cans cream of mushroom
  soup
1 small can sliced mushrooms
  (optional)

2 lbs. potatoes, mashed
1 pkg. frozen peas
½ lb. cheddar cheese, grated
Kitchen Bouquet

1 *Preheat oven to broil. Cook and mash potatoes. Grate cheese.*

2 *In a large frying pan brown onions adding salt and pepper to taste. Add meat and cook thoroughly. Add peas and mushroom soup; color with Kitchen Bouquet. Add sliced mushrooms.*

3 *Place meat mixture in large casserole dish and spread mashed potatoes on top. Sprinkle with cheese and place in oven.*

4 *Broil for about 5 minutes or until slightly brown, and "the best of British Luck."*

LEA THOMPSON (LEONARD)

Corned Beef and Cabbage

½ cup parsley, chopped
1 cup celery, chopped
1 large green pepper, chopped
1 large onion, chopped
1 tsp. garlic powder

1 tbs. cooking oil
1 can corned beef, crumbled
1 to 2 lb. cabbage, cut into 8ths
1 large can tomatoes
¼ cup Worcestershire sauce
salt and pepper, to taste

1 *Saute parsley, celery, green pepper, onion, and garlic powder in oil in a large deep pot for 5 minutes.*

2 *Reduce heat to low. Add corned beef.*

3 *Separate cabbage leaves. Place in pot. Add tomatoes, Worcestershire sauce, salt and pepper. Add enough water to cover cabbage.*

4 *Increase heat and bring to a boil. Reduce heat to medium. Cover and cook for 2 hours and 30 minutes to 3 hours. Serves 4.*

DEE WARD (MIKE)

Beef in the Pot

(meat)
3 lbs. short ribs of beef
3 medium potatoes, quartered
2 small carrots, quartered
1 large can College Inn
   chicken broth

(dumplings)
1½ cups sifted all purposed flour
3 tsp. baking powder
¾ tsp. salt
½ cup milk

1 *Put short ribs in pot and cover with water. Cook for about 2 hours or until meat is tender when tested with a fork.*

2 *Pour off beef broth.*

3 *Add chicken broth to cooked beef and salt and pepper to taste. Bring to a boil.*

4 *Add potatoes and carrots, cook until done.*

5 *For dumplings, sift together flour, baking powder and salt into mixing bowl. Mix in milk with a fork to make a soft dough, stirring as little as possible.*

6 *Drop dough by teaspoon into boiling broth. Keep boiling and cook dumplings for 10 minutes uncovered; then cover pan tightly and boil for 5 minutes longer. Serve with rye bread and radish. Serves 4.*

LINDA LESLIE (PERRY)

Meat Loaf

¾ cup applesauce
1 cup corn flake crumbs
2 tsp. salt
2 tbs. onion, chopped

2 lbs. ground beef
1 cup milk
1 tsp. dry mustard
3 tbs. brown sugar
¼ cup catsup

1 *Combine applesauce, corn flake crumbs, salt, onion, beef and milk and form in loaf in baking dish.*

2 *Mix catsup, mustard, and brown sugar in small bowl. Pour on top of loaf. Bake 1 hour in 350° oven.*

**"Perry likes sweet potatoes baked in jackets on
oven rack with this."**

ROSE ELDER (LEE)

Ham and Shrimp Rolls

1½ cup ham hock, cooked
   and ground (save stock)
⅓ cup uncooked rice
1 pkg. frozen baby shrimp in
   their own juice
12 to 14 cabbage leaves
2 eggs, beaten

¼ cup chives, chopped
¼ cup green peppers, chopped
Accent
¼ tsp. marjoram
¼ tsp. white pepper
½ cup white wine

1 *Cook rice in 1 cup ham stock for 30 minutes.*

2 *Steam cabbage leaves in vegetable steamer or colander for 5 minutes or until just tender. Do not overcook. Remove from heat and place aside. Sprinkle with Accent.*

3 *Drain shrimp (saving juice) and combine with ham, rice, eggs, chives, pepper, marjoram, and green pepper. Toss lightly to mix well.*

4 *Place cabbage leaves on flat surface and add a good amount of the mixture in the center of each cabbage leaf. Fold in the sides and fold the centers together over mixture. Place in casserole dish.*

5 *Combine rest of ham hock stock with shrimp juice and wine. Pour over cabbage rolls. Bake in preheated oven at 375° for 25 minutes or until heated thoroughly. Serves 6.*

RACHEL WADKINS (LANNY)

Meatloaf

1½ lb. ground chuck
1 egg
1 small can tomato sauce
1 tsp. horseradish
⅓ cup bread crumbs, seasoned

salt and pepper, to taste
1 or 2 large carrots, grated
½ large onion, chopped
¼ cup green pepper, chopped
mozzarella cheese, grated

1 *Mix egg, tomato sauce, horseradish, bread crumbs, salt and pepper, carrots, onions, and green peppers in large bowl.*

2 *Add beef to mixture. Mix well. Form into loaf in loaf baking dish or pan. Top with cheese.*

3 *Bake at 350° for 45 minutes.*

NELLIE WILLIAMS (WILLIE)

Green Pepper Steak

1 tbs. soy sauce
1 garlic clove
¼ cup salad oil
1 lb. round steak
   (cut into 1-inch cubes)
1 green pepper (cut into
   1-inch cubes)

1 large onion, coarsely chopped
½ cup diced celery
1 tsp. corn starch
¼ cup water
2 tomatoes, (cut into eighths)

1 *Mix soy sauce, garlic, salad oil together; pour on the steak and let stand for one hour at room temperature.*

2 *Pour this entire mixture into fry pan and allow meat to brown thoroughly on all sides.*

3 *To this, add the pepper, onion, celery. Cover and simmer 5 to 10 minutes over low heat, until vegetables are tender.*

4 *Stir in corn starch dissolved in water. Stir until this thickens. Add the tomatoes, cover and simmer 5 minutes longer.*

5 *Serve over boiled rice. Yields 4 servings.*

SUSAN WIECHERS (JIM)

Steak Sauce with Wine

1 cup fresh mushrooms, sliced
¼ cup green onion, finely
   chopped
¼ cup butter
4 tsp. cornstarch

1 cup burgundy wine
½ cup water
2 tbs. parsley
¾ tsp. salt
dash of pepper

1 *Cook mushrooms and onions in butter just until tender.*

2 *Blend in cornstarch. Add wine, water, parsley, salt and pepper. Cook and stir until bubbly. Serve over steak. Makes 1½ cups.*

NELLIE WILLIAMS (WILLIE)

Bar-B-Q Ribs

4 lbs. ribs (beef or pork)	1 cup catsup
1 garlic clove	2 tbs. brown sugar
1 large onion, diced	3 dashes of tabasco sauce
2 tbs. butter	½ tsp. dry mustard
1 cup canned tomatoes	2 cups beef stock (or 2 bouillon
1 cup diced celery	cubes dissolved in 2 cups water)
1 cup diced green pepper	salt & pepper to taste

1 *Rub ribs with the cut side of garlic clove.*

2 *Place ribs in a shallow baking pan and roast uncovered for 30 minutes in 350° oven.*

3 *Brown onion in the melted butter in a heavy skillet.*

4 *Add remaining ingredients to the onion and the butter, stir and cover; simmer over low heat for one hour.*

5 *After ribs have roasted for 30 minutes, pour sauce over top and roast for 45 additional minutes, frequently basting. Yields 4 servings.*

JANIE JONES (GRIER)

Meat Loaf

½ lb. ground beef	½ cup milk
2 lbs. ground round steak	2 eggs
1 lb. ground pork	1 cup bread crumbs
¾ cup heavy cream	1 tbs. salt
	½ tsp. pepper

1 *Mix well beef, steak, and pork.*

2 *In a large bowl, mix milk, cream, eggs, salt and pepper. Add bread crumbs and mix again. Add meat and mix well with hands.*

3 *Shape in loaf form in bottom of roaster. Put in oven pre-heated to 425°. Leave ½ hour uncovered.*

4 *Reduce heat to 375°. Add ½ inch boiling water around bottom of pan. Cook 1½ hours longer.*

MARIA FLOYD (RAYMOND)

Country Fried Pork Chops

4 pork chops (1¼-inch thick)   **bread crumbs**
½ lb. bacon strips   **salt & pepper, to taste**
2 eggs   **parsley**
flour   **2 cups heavy cream**

1 *Fry bacon strips in large frying pan until they are crisp. Remove from pan and drain on paper towel.*

2 *Dip pork chops in flour, then in lightly beaten eggs, seasoned with salt, pepper, and parsley. Roll each chop in bread crumbs.*

3 *Brown chops quickly in hot bacon fat, careful not to loosen bread crumbs when turning chops.*

4 *When they are browned on both sides, add 1 cup cream. Cover and simmer until tender (about 35-45) minutes.*

5 *Remove the chops and add the remaining cup of cream to pan. Add bacon, stirring over high heat for 5 minutes. Pour sauce on chops and serve immediately. Serves 4.*

"I serve it with pole beans, corn bread and tossed salad."

KATHY SCHROEDER (JOHN)

Roast Loin of Pork with Sour Cream Sauce

4 to 5 lb. loin of pork   **sweet basil (handful)**
1 lemon   **½ cup sour cream**
salt and pepper, to taste   **¼ cup white wine**

1 *Wipe loin of pork with a damp cloth. Rub it with juice of lemon, salt, pepper, and sweet basil.*

2 *Roast pork in moderate oven (350 degrees) allowing about 35 minutes per minutes per pound, until it is well done.*

3 *Remove the pork to a heated platter. Skim excess fat from the pan, and add the sour cream and white wine to pan. Heat sauce, but do not boil. Season with salt and pepper.*

"We serve with spinach casserole and tossed salad."

NANCY HEARD (JERRY)

Chinese Pepper Steak

1½ lb. top sirloin, thinly sliced	3 tbs. oil
1 large onion, sliced	1 clove garlic, minced
1 large bell pepper, cut in thin strips	3 tbs. soy sauce
1½ cup celery, sliced in strips	2 tbs. all purpose flour
¼ tsp. black pepper	2 beef bouillon cubes
1 tsp. salt	cooked rice
	2 cups water

1 *Slice meat very thin; slice onion, bell pepper and celery into strips.*

2 *In very hot skillet, put oil; add meat and stir briskly until pink color has disappeared. Add one cup water with 1 bouillon cube and 1 tbs. soy sauce. Cover and simmer for 10 minutes.*

3 *Add vegetables, garlic, one more bouillon cube and 1 more cup of water. Simmer covered for 15 minutes.*

4 *In a small bowl, combine 2 tbs. flour, 2 tbs. soy sauce with enough water to make a smooth paste. Add to rest of ingredients and bring to a boil. Serve over rice.*

JACKIE ADAMS (SAM)

Corned-Beef Dinner

3 to 4 lbs. corned beef brisket	2 bay leaves
2 onions, sliced	6 small to medium potatoes, pared
2 cloves garlic, minced	6 small carrots, pared
6 whole cloves	6 cabbage wedges (1 medium head)

1 *Place corned beef in Dutch oven; barely cover with hot water. Add onions, garlic, and seasonings. Cover and simmer for about 1 hour per pound of meat, or until fork tender.*

2 *Remove meat from liquid. Add potatoes and carrots. Cover and bring to a boil. Cook 10 minutes.*

3 *Add cabbage and cook 20 minutes more. Serves 6.*

"To carve corned beef, cut across grain making thin slices. Serve with tossed green salad and Southern corn bread."

ROSE ELDER (LEE)

Steak Diane

4 New York strip steaks,
   trimmed of fat
Season All, garlic salt, to taste
Crushed black pepper corns,
   to taste
8-10 sliced mushrooms (or
   13 oz. can)
4 tbs. butter
3 green onions, chopped

1 tsp. dijon mustard
3 tbs. lemon juice
Dash Worcestershire sauce
¼ cup red wine, medium dry
1 tsp. cornstarch

1 *Season each steak on both sides with Season All, garlic salt, and pepper corns.*

2 *Place in broiler oven and cook until medium rare or desired doneness.*

3 *In a skillet, saute onions in butter. Add mushrooms and saute for about 7 minutes.*

4 *In a mixing bowl, add mustard, lemon juice, Worcestershire sauce, wine and cornstarch and mix until smooth.*

5 *Add mustard sauce to onions and mushrooms, stirring until sauce is slightly thickened. Pour over hot steaks. Serves 4.*

JUDY ERSKINE (RANDY)

Sloppy Joes

1 lb. ground beef
½ cup onions, chopped
¼ cup vinegar
1 tbs. Worcestershire sauce

1 tbs. brown sugar
1 can (12-oz.) tomato sauce
½ cup water
salt, pepper, paprika, to taste

1 *Brown ground beef and onion in skillet.*

2 *Add remaining ingredients. Then salt and pepper to taste, and add a pinch of paprika for coloring.*

3 *Cover and simmer for 45 minutes. (The longer it simmers the better the taste.)*

LEE MORRIS (GREG)

Mei Oven Barbequed Pork Chops

8 loin pork chops
salt and pepper, to taste
garlic powder, to taste
1 tbs. chicken fat

1 can (15-oz.) Hunts Tomato
  Herb Sauce
½ cup maple syrup
⅔ cup tomato juice
Mei Yen seasoning
oregano leaves, crushed

1 *Sprinkle loin chops with salt, pepper and garlic powder on both sides.*

2 *Sear both sides in hot skillet with chicken fat.*

3 *Place chops flat in roasting pan.*

4 *Sprinkle generously with Mei Yen Seasoning and oregano leaves.*

5 *Cover with tomato sauce, maple syrup and tomato juice.*

6 *Place in 250° oven for 1 hour and 45 minutes.*

7 *Remove chops from roaster and place on warm platter.*

8 *Strain off fat and serve remaining sauce in gravy boat.*

**"Just great with a light cheese dish or potato salad, vegetable and
a green leafy salad. It is so easy, quick and delicious."**

PRISCILLA "SCOTTY" SANDERS (DOUG)

Pork Chops with Barbecue Sauce

½ cup onion, minced
1 tbs. margarine
½ cup water
½ cup chili sauce
2 tbs. vinegar
1 tbs. Worcestershire sauce

juice of 1 lemon
2 tbs. brown sugar
2 tbs. prepared mustard
hot pepper sauce, to taste
salt and pepper, to taste
6 thick pork chops

1 *Saute onion in margarine. Add remaining ingredients except pork chops and simmer 15 minutes. Adjust seasoning to taste.*

1 *Place chops on a rack in a roasting pan. Pour sauce over meat and bake, uncovered, in a preheated 350° oven for 1 hour. Serves 6.*

JOYCE DOUGLASS (DALE)

Dale's Mother's Meat Loaf

1 lb. ground beef
¼ to ½ cup onion, chopped
¼ to ½ cup green pepper,
   chopped
1 egg

¼ cup milk
10 saltines
1 can tomato soup
¼ tsp. salt and pepper (to taste)

1 *Beat egg. Add milk and beat again.*
2 *Add onion, green pepper, salt and pepper to egg mixture; then add ground beef.*
3 *Crush crackers and add to mixture (add more milk—enough to make a light soft loaf). Shape in loaf.*
4 *Mix tomato soup with 1 can of milk or water and pour over loaf.*
5 *Bake 2 hours at 350°. Serves 4 to 6.*

"After trying several meat loaf recipes after Dale and I were first married, he finally asked me to get his mother's recipe . . . and here it is!"

ELEANOR ROSBURG (BOB)

Stuffed Pork Chops

1 cup day-old bread, torn in
   pieces
¼ cup celery, chopped
¼ cup onion, chopped
2 to 3 tbs. parsley, chopped

6 rib pork chops, cut at least
   ¾-inch thick
¼ tsp. salt
⅛ tsp. pepper
milk
2 tbs. oil

1 *Make a dressing by combining bread, celery, onion, parsley, salt and pepper. Add just enough milk to moisten.*
2 *Trim excess fat from chops. Cut a pocket in the side of each chop and fill with some of the dressing. Sew up the pockets with coarse thread or fasten with toothpicks.*
3 *Brown chops in hot oil in a skillet. Remove to a baking pan. Pour ¼ cup milk over meat. Cover and bake in a preheated 350° oven for 1 hour. Juices can be thickened with a little flour. Serves 4 to 6.*

ARMEN BOROS (JULIUS)

Hungarian Style Meat Loaf or Meat Balls

1 lb. ground round steak
2 eggs
½ tsp. salt

1 medium onion
¼ tsp. black pepper
4 slices dried bread (soaked and
    drained)

Creamed Tomato Sauce

1 small can tomato sauce
use tomato can of 1½ cans
  water

1 tbs. flour
½ pt. sour cream
1 tbs. sugar

NOTE: *For meat loaf: bake in preheated oven at 350° for 1 hour.*
    For meat balls: fry in heavy skillet with just enough oil to cover pan and keep from
    sticking.

1 *In large mixing bowl, add ground beef, eggs; blend well and add rest of in-*
  gredients.
2 *For meat loaf, shape into desired size and place in baking pan.*
3 *For meat balls, shape into spoon-size balls for frying.*

SAUCE:

1 *In sauce pan on top of stove, add tomato sauce, water and sugar; let this*
  come to a boil.
2 *In mixing cup, blend sour cream with flour until smooth.*
3 *Add to tomato sauce, come to a boil and turn off.*
4 *To be used over meat when serving. Yields 4 servings.*

SUSAN NORTH (ANDY)

Salt Beef

Standing rib roast
5 boxes rock salt

1 *Line large pan with 1 box salt.*
2 *Put roast in fat side down; bury roast in remaining salt.*
3 *Cook at 400° 18 minutes per pound.*
4 *Remove from pan and crack salt off meat.*

NANCY SNEED (ED)

Stuffed Peppers Romanean

4 large green bell peppers,
   cored and seeded
1½ lbs. ground meat loaf mix

½ cup raw rice
salt and pepper to taste

Sauce

3 tbs. bacon grease
3 tbs. flour
2 cups boiling water
1 tbs. sugar
2 tbs. vinegar

Use ½ of 20 oz. bottle of ketchup
1 bay leaf
salt and pepper to taste

1 *Preheat oven to 325°.*
2 *In mixing bowl, combine rice and ground meat mix.*
3 *Stuff peppers, and place in large baking pan. Set aside.*
4 *In heavy skillet add bacon grease and flour, stirring constantly until flour is golden brown.*
5 *Slowly add 2 cups boiling water while stirring, mix well until all lumps are dissolved.*
6 *Add remaining ingredients, bring to a boil.*
7 *Remove from heat and pour over stuffed peppers.*
8 *Place in a preheated oven and cook for 2½ to 3 hours.*
9 *Remove and serve with spoons of sour cream. Yields 4 servings.*

JILL McGEE (JERRY)

Grilled Steak

steak of your choice
soy sauce
garlic salt

1 *Trim steak of excess fat (do not remove all fat).*
2 *Baste on both sides with soy sauce and sprinkle with garlic salt.*
3 *Place on grill and turn frequently until cooked to desired doneness.*

McGee likes his steaks, medium rare, served with Jill's potatoes.

TERYL T. WADKINS (BOBBY)

Pork Chops and Rice

rice, uncooked (enough to
  cover bottom of pan)
1 can cream of mushroom
  soup
square cake pan

3 or 4 pork chops
1 small can of mushrooms or
  fresh mushrooms

1 *Warm soup in a saucepan according to directions. Spread rice on cake pan, so it just covers the bottom.*

2 *Pour part of the soup over the rice. Place pork chops on rice and pour the rest of soup over the pork chops. Put mushrooms on top. Cover the pan with foil and cook in oven at 375° for 1 to 1½ hours. The last 5 to 10 minutes, take the foil off and let brown on top. (Can be left in the oven at 150° with the foil on until you are ready to eat.)*

"Onions, green pepper, or a can of tomatoes can also be added. All are optional. The rest of the meal consists of green beans with crumbled bacon on top and a tossed salad."

"M.K." MAXWELL (BILLY)

Maxwell's Meat Loaf

2 lbs. ground beef (chuck,
  round or rump)
2 cups crushed saltine
  crackers
1 large onion, finely chopped
¼ cup green pepper, chopped
4 large stalks celery, finely
  chopped

2 small eggs, beaten
1 can (16-oz.) stewed tomatoes
1 tsp. garlic salt
1 tsp. celery salt
1 tsp. seasoned salt

1 *Combine all ingredients and mix thoroughly but lightly (mixture should have a soft, fluffy consistency). Shape into an oval loaf and place in a baking dish. Bake in a preheated 325° oven for 1½ to 2 hours.*

CINDY MASSENGALE (RIK)

Chicken Fried Steak

2 lbs. round steak	2 eggs
salt and pepper to taste	1 cup milk
1 cup flour	cooking oil

1 *You can (or have your butcher) trim meat of excess fat, cut ½-inch thick and into individual serving sizes of your choice.*

2 *Place flour into shallow bowl.*

3 *In mixing bowl, beat eggs and milk until well blended.*

4 *Salt and pepper meat and coat each piece with flour.*

5 *In a deep heavy skillet, place enough oil to cover the meat and heat to high temperature.*

6 *Place flour coated meat in egg batter and then into flour—place in hot oil.*

7 *Cook at high temperature turning to brown both sides, turn constantly to prevent sticking.*

LINDA TOEPEL (JOHN)

Sweet and Sour Pork Chops

4 medium size pork chops	1 tbs. soy sauce
1 20-oz. can pineapple	flour for coating chops
chunks	cooking oil
⅓ cup vinegar	4 tbs. brown sugar

1 *Preheat oven to 300°.*

2 *In frying pan place oil and bring to high temperature.*

3 *Flour chops and place in hot oil; brown on both sides—remove and set aside.*

4 *In mixing bowl, add juice from pineapple, vinegar, soy sauce.*

5 *Place chops in deep baking dish. Place one tbs. brown sugar on each chop. Add liquid mixture. Cover and bake for 50 minutes.*

6 *Remove and add pineapple chunks; return to oven for an additional 10 minutes.*

ARMEN BOROS (JULIUS)

Veal Scallopini

(Prepared in Radarange oven)

1 lb. thinly sliced veal
1 garlic clove, minced
¾ cup sliced onions
¼ cup vegetable oil
1 6-oz. can drained
    mushrooms

2 tbs. all-purpose flour
½ tsp. salt
⅛ tsp. white pepper
½ cup water
1 8-oz. can tomato sauce

1 *Preheat 9½-inch browning skillet in Radarange oven 4½ minutes.*
2 *Brown veal in oil and garlic for about 2 minutes, turn veal halfway through cooking time.*
3 *Remove veal and garlic from skillet.*
4 *Stir onions and mushrooms into hot oil, place in Radarange oven for 3 minutes.*
5 *Stir in flour, salt, pepper until well blended; cook for 2 minutes.*
6 *Gradually add tomato sauce and water. Cook 5 minutes, stirring halfway through cooking time.*
7 *Arrange veal in skillet, cook 5 to 6 minutes or until veal is tender. Yields 6 servings.*

SANDY PACE (ROY)

Marinade Flank Steak

1 med. size flank steak—
    4 to 6 pounds
½ cup wine vinegar
1½ cup salad oil
¾ cup soy sauce
¼ cup Worcestershire

⅓ cup lemon juice
2 tbs. dry mustard
2½ tsp. salt
1 tbs. black pepper (ground)
½ garlic cube, minced

1 *Marinade 3 to 5 hours.*
2 *Cook over charcoal.*
3 *Slice very thin, cross grain. Yields 6 servings.*

ALMA GENUS (LLOYD)

Short Ribs of Beef

12-14 ribs
1 can beef bouillon
½ cup burgundy wine
¼ tsp. garlic powder
¼ tsp. powdered oregano

juice from ½ lemon
salt and pepper to taste
dash of Tabasco

1 Trim excess marble fat from meat. In baking pan, grill on top of stove until all sides are brown.

2 Mix all other ingredients in bowl and pour over meat. Cover with aluminum foil. Place in preheated oven 325°-350°; cook for one hour and 45 minutes.

3 Uncover and test for desired tenderness.

4 Place 2 tbs. cooking oil or bacon fat in iron skillet. Brown 2 tbs. flour in fat. Pour in sauce from short ribs; stir constantly. Simmer for about 5 minutes and pour over ribs. Serve with rice or mashed potatoes and green vegetables. Yields 6-8 servings.

MARY HARRIS (LABRON)

Veal in Lemon Sauce

1 lb. medallions of veal,
   pounded as thin as possible
   and cut into 3 x 4-inch
   pieces
¼ cup flour
salt and pepper, to taste

4 tbs. butter
2 tbs. olive oil
2 tbs. lemon juice
2 tbs. parsley
10 slices of lemon

1 Lightly dredge pieces of veal in flour. Season with salt and pepper.

2 Heat 2 tbs. of the butter and oil in a large skillet until bubbling.

3 Brown medallions on each side a minute or two. Do not cook more at one time than can be placed in a single layer. Remove to a warm serving platter.

4 Pour off all fat in pan and add remaining butter, lemon juice, and parsley.

5 Put veal back in pan and heat, spooning lemon sauce over veal. Serve the veal garnished with lemon slices.

MARILYN ZARLEY (KERMIT)

Minute Steak Scramble

(Adapted from Better Homes & Gardens, 1961)

4 cube steaks, cut in julienne
  strips
garlic salt
ginger
cooking oil
2 bell peppers, cut in julienne
  strips

1 large white onion, sliced
1 cup celery, bias-cut
1 tbs. cornstarch
½ cup water
¼ cup soy sauce
2 large tomatoes, cut in eighths

1 *Season meat strips with garlic and ginger.*

2 *Brown meat quickly on all sides in oil. Remove meat from skillet.*

3 *Add enough oil to cook peppers, celery, and onions until slightly tender (not mushy, still crunchy), about 3 minutes.*

4 *Mix cornstarch, water, and soy sauce and add to skillet. Cook and stir until mixture thickens.*

5 *Add meat and tomatoes, cooking just long enough to thoroughly heat tomatoes, but not enough to make them lose their body.*

6 *Serve with hot rice, soy sauce, and a side dish of fresh pineapple chunks.*

GAIL MURPHY (BOB)

Marinated Flank Steak with Mushrooms and Onions

flank steak (½ lb. per person)
Italian salad dressing
fresh sliced mushrooms

onions, sliced
½ stick butter
¼ cup Teriyaki sauce

1 *Have butcher score flank steak, marinate in bottles of Italian salad dressing, enough to completely cover—let stand in refrigerator for three days (turning twice a day).*

2 *Saute mushrooms and onions in butter and teriyaki sauce for 10-15 minutes.*

3 *Cook steak over high heat to desired doneness.*

4 *Garnish with mushrooms and onions before serving.*

KATHRYN SMITH (BOB)

Beef Roll-up's with Sauce

2 lbs. top round (thinly sliced)
8 slices of bacon
1 tbs. cooking oil

Sauce

5 8 oz. cans tomato sauce
1 onion, chopped
2 cups hot water
2 tsp. beef flavor base

3 to 4 tsp. minced parsley
1½ tsp salt
1 tsp. thyme

1 *You prepare beef strips or have your butcher cut strips into 2½ x 9-inch sizes and slice in half lengthwise.*

2 *Place a piece of bacon on beef strip and roll up, securing them with thread or tooth picks.*

3 *In heavy skillet, place oil and brown on both sides, remove and place in baking dish; set aside.*

4 *In same skillet pour water and let come to a boil, add remaining ingredients and allow to come to boil.*

5 *Pour enough sauce over beef roll-ups to completely cover. Place in oven and bake at 375° for one hour, uncovered. Remove cover and bake an additional ½ hour or to desired doneness.*

NOTE: Extra sauce can be used to pour over cooked noodles.

NOEL BLANCAS (HOMERO)

Glazed Canadian Bacon

3 to 4 lbs. Canadian bacon
orange slices
whole cloves
⅔ cup cider or apple jack
brandy

½ cup molasses
½ cup brown sugar
1 tsp. dry mustard

1 *Preheat oven to 325°, place bacon in shallow baking pan and bake for 45 minutes, remove and garnish with orange slices and whole cloves.*

2 *Mix cider or brandy, molasses, sugar and mustard.*

3 *Pour mixture over bacon and bake an additional 50 minutes, remove and slice thin strips. Yields 8 servings.*

"This I serve with my cinnamon sticks."

VII

Poultry & Game

Editor's Note

POULTRY AND GAME

*One of the easiest dishes for me to prepare
and do elegantly with little effort is chicken. I
love cooking with wines and vegetables and
chicken breasts take on a classical style when
using grapes, shrimps, mushrooms, chives like
the orange sauce does for duck.*

*On my Chicken in Wine recipe, make the
wine Johannesburg Riesling.*

LINDA WATSON (TOM)

Wild Quail

1 medium size quail	1 pat butter
3 strips bacon	Lawry salt and pepper, to taste

1 *Wrap quail breast with bacon (to keep it moist). Season with Lawry salt and pepper. Place butter on top of quail and put in 325° oven.*

2 *Cook for approximately 40 minutes, basting frequently to prevent drying out. Remove bacon and put under broiler for 10 seconds to brown.*

"Delicious! We enjoy it with a crisp salad and fresh green beans. And Tommy is full and proud to have eaten the game he shot!"

BETTY FORD (GERALD)

Baked Turkey Casserole

4 tbs. butter or margarine	1 tbs. parsley, chopped
2 medium green peppers, cut in strips*	½ tbs. Worcestershire sauce
6 tbs. flour	salt, to taste
3 cups hot chicken stock	¼ tsp. ground white pepper
1 lb. cooked turkey, cut in strips*	1 cup milk
¼ lb. smoked Virginia ham, cut in strips*	10 oz. thin noodles
	2 tbs. cheese, grated
	6 saltine crackers, crushed

all strips should be julienne cut

1 *Melt butter or margarine in 3-quart saucepan. Add green pepper and simmer uncovered for 5 minutes. Add flour and stir well. Add chicken stock and bring sauce to boil.*

2 *Cook sauce for 5 minutes or until smooth. Add turkey, ham, parsley, Worcestershire sauce, salt, and white pepper. Bring to a second boil and add milk gradually while gently stirring. Simmer 5 minutes.*

3 *Cook noodles 7 minutes and drain. Place in a greased shallow casserole dish. Bake in 375° oven for 20 minutes or until lightly browned.*

ROSE ELDER (LEE)

Capon Stuffed with Ground Veal

1 5-lb. whole dressed capon
1 lb. lean veal, finely ground
2 eggs
8 tbs. salted butter
1½ lb. sausage meat, ground
1½ cup dry bread crumbs
(seasoned or plain)

1 medium onion, finely chopped
1 tsp. garlic, finely chopped
2 tsp. Italian seasoning
¼ tsp. ground white pepper
½ cup white wine
1 medium green pepper, finely chopped
¼ tsp. celery salt (or fresh celery,
finely chopped)

1 Wipe inside of capon with paper towel. Set aside.

2 Mix veal, eggs and wine. Set aside for a moment.

3 Melt butter in pan and add bread crumbs. Cook until golden brown.

4 In a large bowl, combine the browned bread crumbs with sausage meat, onions, garlic, and pepper. (Usually mixed by hand.) Add rest of seasonings and gently but thoroughly add the veal mixture.

5 Stuff capon completely with this mixture. Bake at 350° for 1½ hours or until tender.

TALLY MARR (DAVE)

Chicken Sauce Piquant

1 large fryer chicken, cut up
1 large can tomatoes
4 large onions, chopped
½ green bell pepper, chopped

2 cans mushrooms
1 can Le Seur peas
3 cooking spoons of oil
3 cooking spoons of flour

1 Make a roux of oil and flour in a skillet over medium heat. Add chopped onions and pepper to already-browned roux and simmer until onions are clear. Add canned tomatoes.

2 Add cut-up fryer and cover skillet. Do not add water. It will look thick but the chicken will make its own juice.

3 Simmer until the meat is literally falling off the bone. Add drained peas and mushrooms just before serving, and serve over rice.

BRENDA DENT (JIM)

Chicken-n-Rice

8 to 10 chicken wings	1 to 3 chicken bouillon cubes
1 to 2 cups of rice, uncooked	¼ tsp. Accent
½ cup bell pepper, chopped	¼ tsp. seasoned pepper
½ cup celery, chopped	1 to 2 bay leaves
½ cup onion, chopped	salt and pepper, to taste

1 *In a large pot, add chicken wings, onion, bell pepper, celery, seasoned pepper, bay leaf, Accent and bouillon cubes. Cover with water and boil until tender.*

2 *When chicken is tender, remove from pot leaving water mixture.*

3 *Measure two cups of water mixture to each cup of uncooked rice you use. Bring rice and water mixture to a boil in uncovered pot.*

4 *Turn heat to low and cover rice. Add chicken wings and cook over low heat until rice is dry to personal preference. Add salt and pepper.*

SUZANNE MAHAFFEY (JOHN)

Chicken Spaghetti

2 to 3-lb. fryers	1 medium onion, chopped
14 oz. spaghetti	1 can mushrooms
1 large can tomatoes, drained	1 large bud garlic, chopped
1 can tomato soup	1 cup green or ripe olives, sliced
2 cups celery, chopped	¾ lb. cheddar cheese, grated

1 *Salt and pepper fryers and boil in water until tender.*

2 *Remove chicken from broth and cool.*

3 *Remove excess fat from broth and cook spaghetti in broth until tender. Add tomatoes, tomato soup, chopped celery, chopped onion, olives, mushrooms and garlic.*

4 *Cut chicken into bite size pieces and add to spaghetti mixture.*

5 *Place all ingredients in baking dish. Top with cheese.*

6 *Bake at 325° for 30 to 40 minutes. Serves 6-8.*

"I like to serve dinner rolls with the spaghetti, too!"

SHERYL LOTT (LYN)

Chicken

4 large chicken breasts
1½ sticks of butter
½ tsp. oregano
½ tsp. salt
½ tsp. seasoned salt

½ tsp. pepper
½ tsp. garlic salt
½ tsp. celery salt
½ tsp. poultry seasoning
½ tsp. onion salt
½ tsp. paprika

1 *Sprinkle both sides of chicken breasts with oregano, salt, pepper, seasoned salt, paprika, onion salt, garlic salt, celery salt and poultry seasoning.*

2 *Put chicken in casserole dish and slice butter over top. (Place chicken with bone side up.) Bake covered for 1½ hours at 250°.*

IRENE BURNS (GEORGE)

Chicken B & C

1 stick butter
tarragon and thyme, to taste
coarsely ground black pepper, to taste
8 chicken cutlets (boned chicken breasts split lengthwise — each breast makes 2 cutlets)

2 medium white onions, chopped
½ head celery, chopped
2 eggs, *yolks only*
⅓ cup heavy cream
¼ cup water

1 *Melt ¾ stick butter in skillet over medium heat. Brown chicken cutlets, turning only once. After turning, sprinkle to taste with tarragon, thyme and pepper.*

2 *Remove chicken. Place in baking dish, and preheat oven to 350°.*

3 *In remaining butter (add more if necessary), saute onions and celery (approximately 10 minutes). When almost done, lower heat.*

4 *In bowl, combine egg yolks, cream, and water. Beat well.*

5 *When well-blended, add to celery and onions. Heat together. When sauce and vegetables are well-combined, spoon evenly over chicken in baking dish.*

6 *Bake in 350° oven for 25 minutes. May be served over noodles or rice.*

"Recipe is great for company as it multiplies well and may be prepared ahead, then baked for last 25 minutes prior to serving. I usually serve with a salad."

ROSE ELDER (LEE)

Baked Chicken in White Wine

1 good size frying chicken,
   cut up
¾ bottle white wine
1 green pepper, diced
1 bunch chives, diced

1 clove garlic, minced
1 tsp. Season All
1 tsp. seasoned pepper
1 cup fresh mushrooms, sliced
1 tbs. margarine or butter

1 Wash chicken and pat dry with paper towel. Place in casserole dish.

2 Mix Season All, pepper, garlic and sprinkle over chicken. Layer with mushrooms, chives and peppers. Pour wine over this and put butter or margarine on top.

3 Cover with foil, let sit in refrigerator or on counter top for 4-5 hours.

4 When ready to cook, place in preheated oven. Cook at 350° for 45 minutes or until tender.

*"Chicken is a fast dish to cook and if you have the time to
let it marinate in the wine a few hours, it really soaks
up the flavor. When I am at home I also sprinkle a little
beef flavored bouillon over the top. Yields 4 normal servings;
when I have other golfers in, I double the recipe. I serve
with rice or noodles and fresh broccoli. (When on the road,
if a kitchen is available I prepare this dish and let it sit while
I walk the golf course. In areas like Greensboro, vegetables
are fresh and a kitchen is always available.)."*

LINDA LESLIE (PERRY)

Chicken with Duck Sauce

2 or 3-lb. broiler, cut up
8 oz. Russian dressing

2 envelopes onion soup mix
8 oz. apricot jam

1 Place chicken in open roasting pan.

2 Mix all other ingredients together and spread over chicken.

3 Bake 2 hours uncovered at 300°. (For easy clean-up, line roasting pan with heavy foil.)

SANDY HILL (MIKE)

Chicken and Pea Pods

¾ cup onions, coarsely
   chopped
1 clove garlic, minced
½ cup celery, sliced
1 can condensed cream of
   mushroom soup
1 chicken, cut up
⅓ cup flour

¼ cup dry sherry
1 6-oz. can sliced mushrooms
   (1 cup)
1 5-oz. can water chestnuts,
   drained and thinly sliced
1 7-oz. pkg. frozen pea pods
¼ cup oil

1 *Coat chicken with flour. Salt and pepper to taste. Brown in oil. Remove chicken.*

2 *In same oil, cook onions, celery, and garlic until tender. Blend in soup and sherry. Add mushrooms and water chestnuts.*

3 *Return chicken to skillet. Cover and simmer 20 minutes.*

4 *Add pea pods. Cover and simmer 10 minutes. Serve with rice, sauce spooned over chicken and rice.*

"Chinese food is one of our favorites and this is one that the children eat, because it's easy to 'pick out' the pea pods."

DIANNE CRAWFORD (RICHARD)

Cajun Duck

3 ducks
½ stalk celery, chopped
1 medium bunch green
   onions, chopped
1 large white onion
4 cloves garlic, minced

1 bell pepper, chopped
salt and pepper, to taste
red pepper, to taste
¼ cup flour
1 cup sherry

1 *Salt and pepper duck heavily both inside and out, rubbing in by hand.*

2 *Place in heavy Dutch oven, breast up. Sprinkle with more black pepper and salt and a light amount of red pepper. Sprinkle with flour.*

3 *Liquify vegetables in blender with sherry. Pour carefully around the side of ducks. Pour in water enough to cover duck. Cover and cook at 350° for 4 hours.*

RACHEL WADKINS (LANNY)

Chicken Dumplings

(sauce)	*(dumplings)*
1 can (10½-oz.) cream of chicken soup (undiluted)	1½ cup cubed cooked chicken (3 breasts)
1 can (10½-oz.) golden mushroom soup (undiluted)	½ cup celery, chopped
1¼ cup water	1 tsp. parsley
½ cup green peppers, chopped	¼ tsp. pepper, chopped
1 tbs. onion, chopped	¼ tsp. pimento
	1 can buttermilk biscuits, uncooked

1 *Mix chicken soup, mushroom soup, water, green pepper, and onions in casserole dish and simmer on stove.*

2 *In mixing bowl, combine chicken, celery, parsely, pepper and pimento.*

3 *Roll out each biscuit and place about 1 tbs. of chicken mixture in center. Fold over and bring up ends to seal tightly.*

4 *Place in sauce, seam side down, and steam with cover for 15 to 20 minutes. Makes 10 dumplings.*

MARY HARRIS (LABRON)

Baked Parsley Chicken

1 2-lb. chicken	⅛ cup flour
½ cup white wine	1 tbs. water
parsley sprigs	1 tsp. black pepper
	vegetable oil (about 3 tsp.)

1 *Add 1 tsp. black pepper to a small amount of flour. Mix in 1 tsp. vegetable oil and brush over chicken.*

2 *Place chicken in casserole dish and place in oven.*

3 *Bake about 40 minutes at 350˚.*

4 *Mix 2 tsp. vegetable oil with 1 tbs. water, white wine, and baste several times during cooking. Serve with parsley sprigs. Serves 4.*

LINDA WATSON (TOM)

Wild Duck and Sweet Sauce

(duck)	*(sauce)*
2 ducks	Even measurements of:
1 apple, quartered	butter
1 onion, quartered	currant jelly
2 strips bacon	sherry
Lawry salt, salt and pepper,	duck juice
to taste	cornstarch, as needed
1 clove fresh garlic	

1 *Soak the ducks in salt water overnight.*

2 *When ready to cook, preheat oven to 275°.*

3 *Press garlic to get the juice out. Take the two ducks and put 3 or 4 dashes of fresh garlic juice in each.*

4 *Place apples and onions in cavity of ducks and season outside with Lawry salt, salt and pepper.*

5 *Wrap bacon strips around the breasts of the ducks to keep them moist.*

6 *Put one inch of water in a roasting pan with cover.*

7 *Wrap the ducks individually, water tight, but loosely with the silver foil. (Ducks expand in cooking—that is why they must be loose.) Cook for four hours in a 275° oven.*

8 *To prepare sauce, place butter, jelly, sherry and duck juice in double boiler. Heat well, adding cornstarch to thicken as desired. Stirring well, allow to cook for 15 minutes.*

"If you want them to be brown and crisp, put them under the broiler before serving, for just a minute. Remove the apple and onion and throw away before serving. They are only used for flavor and to absorb the fat. Serve with the sweet sauce on the side."

JIMMYE AARON (TOMMY)

Chicken Breasts

6 to 8 chicken breasts
1 can mushroom soup
1 4-oz. can mushroom
   pieces, drained
4 tbs. lemon juice

¼ cup water
paprika
salt and pepper, to taste
margarine

1 *Sprinkle chicken breasts with salt and pepper. Brown breasts on both sides in just enough margarine to keep chicken from sticking.*

2 *Add water and pour lemon juice over the breasts.*

3 *Cover and cook in 350° oven for 45 minutes.*

4 *Remove breasts from skillet or dish and add mushroom soup to the broth.*

5 *Return breasts skin side up to skillet. Sprinkle with paprika and add mushrooms. Cover and cook 20 minutes longer or until very tender. Serve with yellow rice.*

MARY HARRIS (LABRON)

Chicken Mandarin

1 chicken, quartered
2 tbs. vegetable oil
4 tbs. lemon juice
2 tbs. margarine
2 tbs. honey

½ cup orange juice
½ tbs. soy sauce
½ tsp. powdered ginger
1 small can mandarin oranges

1 *Wash and dry chicken pieces carefully. Dust lightly with seasoned flour.*

2 *Saute the chicken in a mixture of margarine and vegetable oil until lightly browned.*

3 *In a separate bowl, mix lemon juice, orange juice, honey, soy sauce, powdered ginger and mandarin oranges.*

4 *Pour this sauce over the chicken and simmer gently in a covered pan for about 30 minutes or until tender. Serves 4.*

W. REID THOMPSON
(Chairman of Board — Pepco)

Roast Duck

3 wild ducks
1 tbs. salt
1 tbs. baking soda
2 cooking apples
1 cup raisins
4 stalks celery, sliced
3 strips bacon
1 small onion, quartered

3 tbs. margarine
½ cup water
salt and pepper, to taste
peel from 1 orange, shredded
1 cup white wine
1 small can concentrated orange
   juice
2 tbs. orange marmalade
1 tbs. cornstarch

Note: One large goose may be substituted for the wild ducks.

1 *Preheat oven to 325°.*

2 *Soak ducks whether frozen or fresh in cold water with salt and soda for 2 hours.*

3 *Pat dry with towel then stuff with sliced apples and raisins.*

4 *Close opening with toothpicks and place in shallow pan, breast up. Salt and pepper well. Place celery and onion in bottom of pan and place bacon strips on breast of birds. Put water and shortening in bottom of pan.*

5 *Cook uncovered first hour, covered with foil the second hour. Then remove foil the third hour. Baste every 20 minutes while uncovered. Add water if necessary.*

6 *For orange sauce, place drippings from roast in saucepan. Add shredded orange peel, wine and orange juice.*

7 *Mix one tablespoon cornstarch with some drippings to make paste and add to above. Then add two tablespoons of orange marmalade.*

"Serve wild duck sliced accompanied by warm sauce. Garnish roast platter with fresh orange slices."

ELSIE FRAZIER TREVIDI (ARMIT)

Broccoli and Chicken Casserole

1 cup mayonnaise
2 cans condensed cream of
   chicken soup
dash curry powder
dash lemon juice

½ cup grated cheese
2 slices thin-sliced bread, cut in
   small squares
4 chicken breasts, boiled
1 bunch broccoli, half-cooked
butter

1 *For sauce, mix together mayonnaise, soup, curry powder and lemon juice.*

2 *Place broccoli in bottom of baking casserole. Break chicken into chunks and place on top of broccoli.*

3 *Pour sauce over broccoli and chicken. Sprinkle with grated cheese.*

4 *Place bread squares on top. Pour enough melted butter to cover bread squares.*

5 *Bake at 450° about 30 minutes.*

ALMA GENUS (LLOYD)

Chicken a la Genus

2 frying chickens, quartered
salt and pepper
paprika
juice of one lemon
1 tsp. leaf oregano
½ tsp. garlic powder

½ cup celery, chopped
½ cup green pepper, chopped
½ onion, chopped
2 cups chicken broth (or the
   equivalent in bouillon cubes)
1 cup sauterne wine

1 *Wash and pat dry chicken and place in shallow baking pan. Brush with melted butter. Add salt and pepper and sprinkle lightly with paprika.*

2 *Place in 400° oven and bake until golden brown. Remove from oven.*

3 *In bowl, mix lemon juice, oregano, garlic powder, chicken broth and wine.*

4 *Pour over chicken. Cover baking pan with aluminum foil. Reduce heat to 325° and return pan to oven. Cook 30 minutes.*

5 *Remove and add cut-up vegetables. Cover again and return to oven. Cook for about 20 minutes until vegetables are just transparent. Thicken broth if desired.*

6 *Serve with baked macaroni and cheese and fresh broccoli or brussel sprouts. Yields 6 servings.*

LEE MORRIS (GREG)

OB's Fried Chicken

6 breasts	3 cups flour
6 thighs	1 tbs. pepper
6 legs	1½ tbs. salt
2 eggs	1 tbs. garlic powder
⅔ cup half and half milk	1 stick butter
beer (enough to cover chicken)	2 cups safflower oil

1 *Remove skin from chicken and wash. Marinate in shallow pan for a couple of hours with enough beer to cover chicken.*

2 *Into a measuring cup place 2 eggs; add enough milk to make 1 cup. Pour into shallow bowl and mix well. Set aside.*

3 *Into double brown paper bag place flour, pepper, salt, garlic powder. Shake well.*

4 *Heat in large electric skillet (400° heat must be maintained during entire preparation) butter, safflower oil.*

5 *Drain chicken on paper towels and pat until slightly dry. Dip pieces in egg mixture and place into bag of flour and shake well (do not crowd chicken in bag). Shake off excess flour and place in hot oil. Repeat process until skillet is full.*

6 *Fry chicken for 10 minutes at 400° uncovered; cover for 5-10 minutes more or until it is golden brown around the edges. Turn with tongs (no fork please!). Fry other side for 5-8 minutes uncovered, then cover and fry 5-8 minutes longer. Remove cover and turn chicken one more time allowing it to get crisp and brown (3-4 minutes).*

7 *Remove from skillet and drain on paper towels. Place chicken in shallow pan or roaster, uncovered. Dot with butter and place in oven at warm temperature until ready to serve, but do not let dry out in oven.*

"My family just loves my fried chicken and I always fry this amount at one time. Although our daughter is away at school, I still prepare the same amount, so that when Greg wants to snack it is there for him (if the kids don't beat him to it)."

CINDY CURL (ROD)

Venison Italiano

2 lbs. venison (veal may be
   substituted)
2 eggs, slightly beaten

flour
salt and pepper

1 *Prepare venison by slicing approximately ¼ inch thick; salt and pepper both sides.*

2 *Dip cutlets in slightly beaten egg, then in flour.*

3 *Fry pieces in cooking oil until thoroughly cooked. Drain on paper towel.*

4 *Arrange the cooked venison in baking pan.*

5 *Cover with sauce; top with thin slices of Mozzarella cheese. Bake at 350° until cheese melts and begins to bubble. Serve hot. Complement with spaghetti (same sauce), garlic bread and salad.*

Tomato Sauce

1 clove garlic
3 tbs. olive oil
1 whole clove
½ lb. hamburger
2 carrots, finely diced

celery leaves
1 medium onion
1 large can peeled Italian
   tomatoes
2 small cans tomato paste

1 *Pan fry garlic and clove in olive oil; add hamburger, salt and pepper; brown meat. Remove garlic and clove.*

2 *Strain in can tomatoes; add tomato paste, onion, celery leaves, carrots.*

3 *Simmer, stirring occasionally for 3 to 4 hours—the longer the better. The sauce will taste better the longer it cooks.*

OLIVIA CHRISTOPHE
(Sister to Donald Swalens of Brussells)

Waterzooi a la Gantoise

1 kgm. (2.2 lbs.) bones	2 onions
½ kgm. (1.1 lbs.) skin of beef	5 to 6 leeks
3 litres (3 qts. + 9 tbs.) water	1 stalk celery
bouquet garni**	1 carrot
1 stewing chicken	roux*

*"A 'roux' in my dictionary is brown-butter sauce — brown sauce."
**Bouquet garni — a bunch of parsley, thyme, laurel or other aromatic plants.

Roux: Make roux with 40 grams (a little over 1 oz.) flour and 2 litres (2 qts. + 6 tbs.) stock.

1 Prepare stock with bones, skin of beef and bouquet garni.
2 Cook chicken in stock until tender.
3 Chop onions, leeks, celery and carrot into very small pieces (or put through blender). Let them sweat for about 10 minutes in a little butter.
4 Add to chicken.
5 Remove chicken from stock when cooked, cut into portions and keep warm. Strain stock.
6 Make roux, add to stock. Add vegetables. Thicken stock with egg yolks beaten into cream. Season to taste with salt and pepper; add chopped parsley and chervil. Put chicken into a warm soup tureen; cover with sauce and serve with bread and butter. Yields 4 servings.

MARGARET LEWIS (BABE)

Margaret's Crispy Duck with Orange Sauce

two 5-6 lb. ready to cook ducklings
salt and pepper
3 tbs. butter, or spray bottom of roaster with cooking ease

1 *Melt butter in roasting pan (or spray with cooking ease).*

2 *Wash ducklings inside and out, dry thoroughly with paper towel. Season ducks with salt and pepper inside cavities and out.*

3 *Roast uncovered in preheated oven at 475° turning ducks on both sides (I usually start them on their sides) about 25 minutes on each side—total cooking time about 1 hour and 20 minutes. Prick the skin in a few places on the lower breasts and sides to release fat. This allows duck to become more crispy.*

4 *When ¾ done, pour off excess grease. Return to oven and complete roasting.*

5 *Quarter and serve (some people like to bone and serve).*

NOTE: I never prick the top of breasts and legs—this tends to dry out the meat.

Orange Sauce

⅔ cup brown sugar, tightly packed	**2 tbs. grated orange rind**
⅔ cup granulated sugar	**2 cups orange juice**
2 tbs. cornstarch	**rind of ½ orange finely shredded lengthwise**

1 *Combine all ingredients in saucepan; simmer until clear and slightly thickened, about 4 minutes. Serve on side with duck. A beautiful complement with this crisp and tasty duck—simple but elegant—I always serve this orange sauce with my duck.—Rose Elder.*

"Margaret Lewis is the wife of 'Babe' Cleney Lewis, a brother pro-tem to the Elders and a longtime golfing companion."

CONNIE WHITAKER (LOVELL)

Chicken with Stuffed Olives, Tunisian (Pouletaux Olives Farcies)

4 whole chicken breasts, split, boned, salt and black pepper.

½ tsp. ground cumin
3 cups minced onion
¾ cup chopped pimento-
   stuffed olives
½ cup snipped parsley
3 cloves garlic, minced
2 tbs. lemon juice
¼ tsp. sugar
32 pimento-stuffed olives
   parsley, if desired

24 small, new potatoes, cooked
   and skinned (do not overcook)
2 tbs. olive oil or vegetable oil
2 tbs. butter or margarine
⅓ cup olive oil or vegetable oil
½ cup butter or margarine
1 tsp. salt
¾ tsp. paprika
½ tsp. crushed red pepper

1 *Make chicken meatballs (see below). Sprinkle chicken breasts with salt, black pepper and ½ tsp. cumin. Heat 2 tbs. oil and 2 tbs. butter in a large skillet until hot.*

2 *Brown chicken breasts in oil and butter; arrange in a single layer in roasting pan. Brown chicken meatballs in oil and butter in skillet (add more oil if needed); place in roasting pan with chicken breasts. Heat ⅓ cup oil and ½ cup butter in skillet until hot. Saute onions in oil mixture until tender.*

3 *Stir in remaining ingredients, except olives and cooked potatoes, into onions. Spoon onion mixture over chicken in roasting pan; add olives and potatoes, cover. (NOTE: dish can be prepared to this point 24 hours in advance— cover and refrigerate. Just proceed with next step, increasing baking time to 40 minutes).*

4 *Heat oven to 375°. Bake chicken 25 minutes; remove cover. Add cooked potatoes. Bake until hot, about 5 minutes longer. Arrange chicken breasts, meatballs and hot potatoes on platter. Spoon onion mixture over chicken. Garnish with parsley.*

Chicken Meatballs (recipe follows):

Chicken Meatballs (makes 2 dozen)

¾ lb. ground cooked chicken* snipped parsley
½ cup fine bread crumbs 1 tbs. water
1 egg, beaten ¼ tsp. salt
1 tbs. grated onion ⅛ tsp. ground cumin
⅛ tsp. pepper

Can substitute turkey, or ground lean beef mixed with veal for ground chicken.

1 *Mix all ingredients; shape into 1-inch balls.*

"When Lovell and I entertained the golfers, they really raved about this. I like it because you can prepare it the day before and it tastes delicious when you take it from the oven for serving; it's colorful and attractive also."

SOOZI PATE (JERRY)

Peachy Oven Fried Chicken

1 2½ to 3 lb. broiler-fryer 2 tbs. margarine or butter
  chicken, cut into pieces 2 tbs. salad oil
⅔ cup flour 1 can (29 oz.) yellow cling peach
1 tsp. salt halves, drained

1 *Rinse chicken. Pat dry.*
2 *Combine flour, ginger and salt.*
3 *Dredge chicken in flour mixture.*
4 *Melt margarine with oil in shallow baking pan.*
5 *Arrange chicken skin side down in pan. Do not stack pieces. Bake at 350° for 15 minutes. Yields 4-6 servings.*

"Peachy Oven Fried Chicken" is a delicious combination of ginger, peaches and chicken."

NOTES

VIII

Rice, Pasta, Beans & Grain

WALTER PITTS*

Chili

¼ cup olive oil
2 lbs. lean chili meat
1 tsp. salt
1 tbs. ground camino seed
3 cups water

½ tsp. black pepper
1 tsp. cayenne pepper
6 tbs. chili powder
3 tbs. massa (or flour)

1 Sear chili meat in ¼ cup olive oil in thick saucepan until it turns grey (don't brown).

2 Add all other ingredients, except water, while stirring. Stir in well.

3 Add 3 cups water and cook slowly over low flame until meat is tender. If it thickens too much, add a little more water.

4 This chili may be served over pinto beans, spaghetti, or rice. "Chili originated in Texas, although it is generally referred to as a Mexican dish. A real Texan-Mexican does not use tomatoes in chili; the tomato was added in the American version."

*Walter Pitts is a Business Car Chef with the Southern Pacific Railroad and loves to prepare a meal with lobster for Lee and Rose, to which he adds his special touch.

"I enjoy cooking for Rose and Lee because they are so gracious and 'for real' and always enjoy my food."

MARILYN DERMER (HAROLD)

Farfel

2 pkgs. barley grouts
1 large box fresh mushrooms, diced
2 medium onions, diced
1 tsp. garlic salt

4 stalks celery, diced
3 large tbs. chicken fat
salt and pepper, to taste
1 tsp. Lawry's season salt

1 Cook barley grouts according to directions on package.

2 Saute vegetables in chicken fat about 20 minutes.

3 Blanche cooked grouts and add to sauteed vegetables stirring constantly.

4 Season with Lawry's season salt, garlic salt and pepper. Serve hot.

JOANNE KOHLER (ROY)

Spaghetti and Meat Balls

(sauce)

¾ cup onion, chopped
1 clove garlic, minced
3 tbs. olive oil
2 1-lb. cans tomatoes (4 cups)
2 6-oz. cans tomato paste
  (1⅓ cup)
1 cup water
1 tbs. sugar
1½ tsp. salt
½ tsp. pepper
1½ tsp. crushed oregano
1 bay leaf

(meat balls)

¼ cup Parmesan or Romano
  cheese, grated
4 slices dry bread
2 eggs
2 tbs. parsley, chopped
1 clove garlic, minced
1 tsp. oregano or basil, crushed
1 tsp. salt
dash of pepper
olive oil

1 To prepare meat balls, soak bread in water 2 to 3 minutes then squeeze out moisture. Combine bread with remaining ingredients except olive oil; mix well.

2 Form in small balls (about 20). Brown slightly in hot oil. Set aside.

3 In another skillet, blend the sauce. Cook onion and garlic in hot oil until tender but not brown; stir in remaining ingredients.

4 Simmer uncovered for 30 minutes; remove bay leaf.

5 Add meat balls and cook 30 minutes longer. Serve over spaghetti noodles. Serves 6.

LOUISE NELSON (BYRON)

Grits Souffle

3 cups grits
8 cups water
2 tbs. salt
4 eggs, beaten until light

2 cups cream
1 lb. sharp cheese, grated
1 stick butter
garlic cheese spread, to taste

1 Boil grits in water with salt until thick.

2 Add other ingredients to cooked grits, mixing well.

3 Place grits mixture in baking dish and bake 1 hour at 325°. Yields 12-15 servings.

JUDI GREEN (HUBERT)
Lasagna

1 lb. (5 links) sweet or hot Italian sausage, skinned & chopped
¾ lb. ground beef
½ cup onion, finely chopped
2 cloves garlic, crushed
2 tbs. sugar
1½ tsp. basil
½ tsp. fennel seed
1 tsp. Italian herb seasoning (optional)
¼ tsp. pepper
salt to taste
¼ cup parsley, chopped

1 can (35-oz.) Italian style plum tomatoes
2 cans (6 oz. ea.) tomato paste
1 to 2 (8 oz.) cans herb or onion tomato sauce
½ cup water
12 curly lasagna noodles
1 carton (15-16 oz.) riccotta or cottage cheese (about 2 cups)
1 egg
¾ lb. mozzarella cheese, thinly sliced
¾ cup grated Parmesan cheese

1 *In a 5-qt. Dutch oven, saute sausage, beef, onions and garlic over medium heat, stirring frequently, until well browned, about 20 minutes. Add sugar, basil, fennel seed, Italian seasoning, 1 tbs. salt, the pepper and half the parsley. Mix well. Add tomatoes with their juice, tomato paste, tomato sauce and water. Mash tomatoes with a wooden spoon. Bring to a boil, reduce heat and simmer, covered, until thick, about 1½ hours. Stir occasionally.*

2 *To cook the noodles, bring 3 qts. water and 1 tbs. salt to a boil in an 8-qt. kettle. Add lasagna noodles, two or three at a time. Return to a boil and cook uncovered, 10 minutes or until just tender. Stir occasionally. Drain and rinse with cold water. Drain on paper towels.*

3 *In a medium bowl, combine riccotta cheese with egg, remaining parsley and ½ tsp. salt. Mix well.*

4 *Spoon 1½ cups meat sauce on the bottom of a baking dish, 13 x 9 x 2 inches. Arrange six noodles lengthwise in dish, overlapping to cover. Spread with half the riccotta cheese mixture. Top with a third of the mozzarella slices. Spoon 1 1/12 cups meat sauce over mozzarella and sprinkle with ¼ cup of the Parmesan cheese. Add, in layers, remaining noodles, riccotta cheese mixture, half the remaining mozzarella and the remaining meat sauce. Top with remaining mozzarella. Sprinkle with remaining Parmesan cheese.*

5 *Cover with foil, molding it tightly around edge of dish. Bake in a preheated 375° oven 25 minutes. Remove foil and bake 25 minutes longer or until bubbly. Cool 15 minutes before serving. Serves 6-8.*

"Hubert's favorite dish is lasagna, and I'm sure when Myatt grows up it will be his favorite too. Hubert eats this Italian dish for breakfast, lunch and dinner."

Courtesy of "Five Star Favorites" Dessert Charities, Inc. 1974.

JEANNIE WEISKOPF (TOM)

Curried Wild Rice

1 cup wild rice	½ lb. fresh mushrooms, sliced
1½ cups chicken broth	1 stick butter
¼ cup green onion, chopped	½ tsp. salt
½ cup green pepper, chopped	¼ tsp. black pepper
	1½ tbs. curry powder

1 Rinse wind rice in large bowl of cold water. Drain in either colander or strainer. Repeat this procedure until water stays clear. Let the rice set in cold water while you do the following.

2 Saute vegetables in butter for approximately 5 minutes (or until vegetables are soft).

3 Add rice to vegetables and mix well. Then add seasonings.

4 Pour into 1-qt. casserole dish.

5 Pour chicken broth over rice mixture and stir gently.

6 Cover and bake at 350° for 50 minutes.

"To prepare in advance, do the first 5 steps above
and add broth just before placing in oven."

IREANE REAVES (CALVIN)

Savory Rice

4 strips bacon, diced	2¼ cups water
1 medium onion, chopped	1 beef flavored bouillon cube
½ small green pepper, chopped	½ tsp. salt
	½ tsp. Worchestershire sauce
1 cup raw rice	2 tbs. pimento, diced

1 Fry bacon until crisp. Remove from pan and dice. Save fat.

2 Saute onion and green pepper in bacon fat 2 to 3 minutes or until tender.

3 Add remaining ingredients, stirring until bouillon cube dissolves. Bring mixture to a boil. Stir in bacon.

4 Place mixture in covered baking dish. Bake at 350° for 1 hour or until rice is tender and water is absorbed. Yields 8 servings.

"Calvin Reaves is related to Rose & Lee. He is also Lee's Amateur
Golfing Partner at the Bing Crosby-Pebble Beach Tournament."

JIMMYE AARON (TOMMY)

Bean Casserole

1 pkg. frozen french beans
1 pgk. frozen lima beans
1 pkg. frozen English peas
1½ cups Hellman's
    mayonnaise
1 small can Pet milk

1½ tbs. Worcestershire sauce
1 small onion, finely chopped
1 can water chestnuts, sliced
1 cup bread crumbs
3 tbs. butter

1 Cook vegetables according to directions on package.

2 Drain water off cooked vegetables and mix with all other ingredients in a casserole dish.

3 Top casserole with bread crumbs. Dot with butter and bake at 350° for 30 minutes.

SUSAN NORTH (ANDY)

Green Rice

2 cups rice, uncooked
2 green peppers, finely
    chopped
2 small onions, finely chopped
1 pkg. fresh spinach
2 bunches parsley, finely
    chopped

3 eggs, beaten
2 cups milk
1 lb. cheddar cheese, shredded
⅔ cup Wesson oil
salt and pepper, to taste

1 Cook rice according to directions. Set aside.

2 Pour oil over peppers and onions and let stand one hour.

3 Blend rice, spinach, parsley, peppers, onions, and oil together.

4 Add eggs, milk and season with salt and pepper.

5 Place in oblong casserole dish, using alternate layers of rice mixture and cheese. Bake 1 hour at 350°.

*OTHER WILD RICE RECIPES
—*from Mrs. Julius Boros*

Wild Rice with Sausage

1 *While preparing rice, chop up two good solid green peppers and four small onions. Saute in butter.*

2 *In another frying pan, chop up 1 lb. of hot or medium sausage, cook and drain.*

3 *Mix all ingredients together with wild rice and heat in oven.*

Wild Rice Jambolaya

4 cups prepared wild rice

1 *Saute in ¼ cup fat:*

2 cups finely chopped celery   **8 oz. can mushrooms, drained**
1 chopped onion   **½ lb. pork, cubed**
½ lb. veal, cubed

2 *Combined with drained rice. Add:*

1 can mushroom soup   **½ to ¾ cup water**
(1 tbs. soy sauce optional)

3 *Bake covered at 350° for 2 hours. Very good when reheated.*

ARMEN BOROS (JULIUS)
Wild Rice Dressing

4 cups prepared wild rice   **½ cup cooked giblets and neck**
½ cup giblet stock   **meat, chopped**
4 links or ¼ lb. cooked pork
sausage, crumbled

1 *Saute in fat from sausage:*

2 to 3 tbs. chopped onion   **¼ to ½ cup chopped celery**
1 tbs. chopped green pepper   **2 tbs. salt**
1 tbs. melted butter   **salt and pepper to taste**

2 *Toss ingredients together. Since all ingredients are cooked, dressing can be packed in solidly. If more moisture is needed, use more of giblet stock.*

Optional: Sliced water chestnuts or mushrooms may be added.

Wild Rice Party Recipe

1 cup raw wild rice	1 can mushroom soup
1 can cream of chicken soup	2 small cans mushrooms, drained
2 beef bouillon cubes in	1 tsp. salt
1 cup water	1 bay leaf crumbled
¼ tsp. each celery salt,	¾ cup chopped celery
pepper, onion salt, paprika	6 tbs. chopped onion
1½ lbs. lean ground beef	½ cup slivered almonds

1 *Prepare wild rice and place in casserole. Add soups, mushrooms, water, seasonings, and mix gently.*

2 *Saute onions and celery in butter until transparent. Add to casserole. Brown meat and add. Sprinkle with almonds. Bake, covered, at 350° for 1½ hours. (Add more bouillon if it becomes too dry while baking.)*

This collection reprinted from "Mah-No-Min,"[Munsingwear, Minneapolis, Minnesota].

ROSE ELDER (LEE)

Baked Macaroni and Cheese

1 8-oz. pkg. macaroni, cooked	½ stick margarine or butter
as per package instructions	2 tbs. chopped parsley
2 eggs, slightly beaten	½ tsp. thyme leaves
2 tsp. Season All	1 lb. cheese, grated
2 flavored bouillon cubes	(½ sharp, ½ mild)
(use flavor to complement	1 cup milk
your meal)	

1 *Preheat oven to 375°.*

2 *Cook macaroni as per package directions, adding bouillon cubes to water. Do not overcook.*

3 *Drain and pour in large mixing bowl. Add grated cheese and butter in pieces; toss lightly to mix well. Add eggs and rest of ingredients, being very careful not to beat but fold lightly.*

4 *Pour into casserole dish and bake for 20 minutes or until just bubbly. (You may wish to add more or less milk. I like it better more fluffy than very stiff.)*

Note: I never wash macaroni in cold water before preparing to bake; only drain well.

"A favorite of Irey Hillsman"

JOANNE KOHLER (ROY)

Lasagna Casserole

(filling)

1 lb. Italian sausage
1 clove garlic, minced
1 tbs. whole basil
1½ tsp. salt
1 one-pound can tomatoes
   (2 cups)
2 6-oz. cans tomato paste
10 oz. lasagna or wide noodles

3 cups fresh Riccotta or creamy
   cottage cheese
½ cup grated Parmesan or
   Romano cheese
2 tbs. parsley flakes
2 eggs, beaten
2 tsp. salt
½ tsp. pepper
1 lb. Mozzarella cheese, thinly
   sliced

1 *Brown meat slowly. Spoon off fat and add garlic, basil, salt, tomatoes, and tomato paste. Simmer uncovered ½ hour, stirring occasionally.*

2 *Cook lasagna until tender in large amount of boiling salted water, approximately 10-20 minutes.*

3 *For filling, mix cottage cheese, Parmesan or Romano cheese, parsley, eggs, salt and pepper.*

4 *Place ½ the cooked noodles in a 13 x 9 x 2-inch baking dish. Spread with half the cheese filling. Cover with half the Mozzarella cheese and half the meat sauce. Repeat layers.*

5 *Bake in moderate oven at 375° for 30 minutes. Before cutting in squares, let stand 10-20 minutes so that filling will set slightly. Makes 12-15 servings.*

CLAUDIO TREVINO (LEE)

Chili Beans

1 lb. pinto beans, washed
   thoroughly
1 medium size onion, diced
1 lb. ground round
1 bell or chili pepper, diced

1 lb. sausage meat
2 tsp. red chili powder
salt and pepper to taste
1 tsp. oregano powder
1 tsp. cumin powder

1 *Cover pinto beans with 3 to 4 qts. water, cook over medium heat for approximately 2 hours.*

2 *Add the rest of ingredients and simmer for an additional hour or until beans are tender.*

ROSE ELDER (LEE)

Rose's Lasagna (by special request)

3 tbs. olive oil
1 lb. Italian sweet sausage
(skinned and sliced)
1 lb. ground beef, very lean
¼ lb. ground pork
1 large can or 1 lb. fresh
mushrooms (chopped)
4 garlic cloves, crushed
1 tsp. Italian seasoning
1½ tsp. oregano
1 large size jar Ragu cooking
Italian cooking sauce (21 oz.)

4 tsp. Accent
1 can Ragu tomato sauce or
condensed tomato soup
1 pkg. rippled lasagna noodles
(16 oz.)
1 carton Riccotta cheese
¾ cup Parmesan cheese
3 eggs
1 can cooking tomatoes (10 oz.)
(quartered)

1 *Cook noodles according to directions on package, adding 2 tsp. Accent and 1½ tbs. olive oil.*

2 *Over low heat, add 1½ tbs. olive oil to very large deep skillet or dutch oven (I use my Paella pan). Add ground pork, beef and sliced sausage. Saute, stirring occasionally. Add garlic, Italian seasoning, oregano, Accent and saute about 5 to 6 minutes. Add cooking sauce, tomatoes, mushrooms and simmer over low heat for about 20 minutes while preparing cheese filling.*

3 *For cheese filling, combine Riccotta cheese, mozzarella, parmesan and eggs in mixing bowl. Blend well.*

4 *Place noodle strips in bottom of casserole dish. Spread with layer of meat sauce, then a layer of cheese filling. Repeat until all is used.*

5 *Bake in oven at 350° for ½ hour.*

6 *Heat can tomato soup or sauce and pour over cooked dish.*

HELEN MURCH

Noodle Casserole

1 cup butter or margarine
½ lb. very fine noodles
2 cups instant rice
2 cans onion soup

2 cans chicken broth
1 tsp. soy sauce
1 cup water
2 8-oz. cans water chestnuts, drained and sliced

1 Melt butter in sauce pan. Add uncooked noodles and cook until golden brown, stirring often.
2 Add other ingredients and mix well.
3 Place in 3-qt. casserole dish and bake uncovered at 350° for 45 minutes.

ANGIE LUNN (BOB)

Spanish Rice

1 cup rice, regular (do not use instant)
½ small onion, minced
3 chicken bouillon cubes, dissolved in 1 cup very hot water

1 16-oz. can whole tomatoes
¼ tsp. cumin
salt to taste
2 tbs. oil

1 In about 2 qt. pot add enough oil to cover bottom well, about 2 tbs.
2 Add rice and stir frequently until golden.
3 Add onions, tomatoes; crush tomatoes while stirring in.
4 Add dissolved bouillon cubes, cumin, salt to taste, stir well.
5 Simmer covered over low heat for about 20 minutes, until all liquid is absorbed.
NOTE: You may add some of the tomato juice to your liquid. Yields 4 servings.

DONNA JAMIESON (JIM)

Low Fat-Part Skim Lasagna

2 tbs. cooking oil
1 clove garlic, crushed
1 onion, chopped
2 lbs. ground beef
3 jars Ragu sauce (8 oz. jars)
2 tbs. Worcestershire sauce
3 to 4 pkgs. lowfat mozzarella
  cheese, sliced or chopped
(Kraft makes an excellent low
moisture, part skim mozzarella
cheese.)

2 tsp. garlic salt
1 tsp. each of seasoned salt,
  sugar, oregano and pepper
1 large pkg. lasagna noodles
3 to 4 cups Light n' Lively
  cottage cheese

1 *Heat oil in large skillet. Add onion and garlic. Saute until golden brown. Stir in beef and cook until beef is browned. Add remaining ingredients. Mix well. Simmer 1 hour in sauce pan.*

2 *Cook lasagna noodles in large pot of water for 15 minutes only. Drain well.*

3 *In large baking dish, make layers of meat sauce, cheese, and noodles starting with a little meat sauce on the bottom of the dish. Then add a layer of noodles and a layer of low fat cottage cheese. Sprinkle with parmesan and add chopped low fat mozzarella. Repeat layering until you reach top of dish with cheeses making the final layer. Bake uncovered at 375° for 30-35 minutes.*

**"Serve with lettuce and tomato salad with oil and vinegar
dressing. Also Italian bread with garlic butter."**

NOTES

IX

Salads & Salad Dressings

DOLORES HOPE (BOB)

*Antipasto Salad**

iceberg lettuce, very cold and dry
salami, cut into slivers
mozzarella cheese, diced
marinated artichoke hearts, chilled & drained
Italian pickled peppers (mild peperoncini), chilled and drained
celery hearts and tops, chopped

pimentos, drained and cut into slivers
ripe olives, chilled and drained
anchovies, torn or cut into small pieces (optional)
capers (optional)
fresh parsley, minced (optional)
Parmesan or Romano cheese, grated
Garbanzo beans, chilled and drained

Dressing
salt and coarsely ground black pepper
1 part high-quality Italian wine vinegar
3 parts Italian olive oil

1 *Tear lettuce into bite-size pieces and arrange as a bed in a large chilled salad bowl.*

2 *Arrange individual salad ingredients in wedge-shaped sections on top of lettuce (if using a clear bowl, layer the ingredients). Do not toss.*

3 *Bring to the table to show off the colorful arrangement. Add salt and pepper and vinegar and toss lightly. Add oil and toss salad again.*

Courtesy of "Five Star Favorites", Dessert Charities, Inc. 1974.

HELEN MURCH

Authentic Horcher Sauce

1 pt. mayonnaise
4 oz. chili sauce
⅓ cup brandy

1 oz. dijon mustard
4 dashes Tabasco sauce

1 *Place all ingredients in mixing bowl and whip at slow speed for 5 minutes or until silky smooth.*

VIRGINIA IVERSON (DON)

Seven Layer Salad

1 head lettuce, broken into
   pieces
1 cup green pepper, diced
¼ cup onion, chopped
1 pkg. frozen peas, cooked
   but left firm

1 pt. Miracle Whip salad dressing
3 tbs. sugar
3 tbs. Parmesan cheese
bacon, fried crisp and crumbled
1 cup celery, diced

1 *Into salad bowl, make layers of lettuce, celery, green pepper, onion, frozen peas, alternately, ending with salad dressing. Sprinkle sugar over dressing. Sprinkle parmesan cheese over sugar. Crumble crisp fried bacon over top. Do not stir.*

2 *Cover tightly with plastic wrap and refrigerate. This can be prepared a day (or 8 hours) before serving, just seal tightly.*

CINDY MASSENGALE (RIK)

Berries and Cream Salad

1 large pkg. strawberry jello
1 small can crushed pineapple
1 pt. frozen strawberries

1 small carton sour cream
2 bananas, sliced

1 *Prepare jello* according to directions, substituting fruit juice from the pineapple and strawberries for the cold water. (Add water if not enough juice for the required 2 cups.)*

2 *After mixing, divide jello in half, leaving 2 cups in the container from which you will be serving. Add the bananas and place in refrigerator until firm.*

3 *When jello is firm, spread the surface with the sour cream.*

4 *In separate dish, mix together the strawberries, pineapple and remaining jello. Gently pour this over the sour cream layer and return to the refrigerator until firm. Serve on lettuce or make in a mold.*

"We usually top the meal off with dairy fresh milk straight from the cow, but I guess that is not practical for most of your readers, either!"

ROSE ELDER (LEE)

Slaw

fresh lemon juice, to taste
⅓ cup mayonnaise
1 tbs. fruit juice

⅛ tsp. ginger
1 qt. finely shredded cabbage
½ to ¾ cup fresh or canned fruit
½ cup fresh strawberries, sliced

1 *Combine mayonnaise, lemon juice, fruit juice and ginger. Chill.*

2 *Just before serving, toss cabbage and fruit with mixture until evenly coated. Serves 6.*

LINDA TOEPEL (JOHN)

Lime Jello Salad

1 pkg. lime jello
1 cup boiling water
½ cup cold water

1 pkg. 3-oz. cream cheese,
   softened
1 small can crushed pineapple

1 *Add the undissolved jello to cheese. Next add boiling water, stirring until jello is dissolved and cheese is smooth. Then add cold water.*

2 *Let stand in refrigerator until mixture starts to thicken.*

3 *Add pineapple and pour into mold.*

4 *Just before serving, place molding dish in warm water just until jelled salad separates from side of dish. Turn dish upside down until salad slips out easily. Serve immediately.*

ROSE ELDER (LEE)

Lee's Favorite Quick & Easy Salad Dressing

½ cup mayonnaise
¼ cup catsup

2 tbs. fresh lemon juice
2½ tbs. sugar

1 *In mixing cup, combine all ingredients and blend well. Yields about ¾ cup dressing (enough for 4 salads). Very good on bed of lettuce with mandarin oranges, sprinkled with poppy seeds.*

"I first had this at Marie & Walton Jennings' home.
I've been using it ever since."

GLORIA H. COOK (TOM)
Bean Salad

2 cans green beans
2 cans wax beans
1 can kidney beans
1 can Garbanzo beans

½ cup onion, thinly sliced
1½ white vinegar
½ cup salad oil
1½ cup sugar
salt and pepper, to taste

1 *Drain and wash beans in colander, washing kidney beans separately.*
2 *Heat sugar and vinegar until sugar dissolves. Let cool.*
3 *Add salad oil to vinegar mixture and pour over beans.*
4 *Marinate at least overnight.*
5 *Drain well before serving. Mixture will keep 2 or 3 weeks in refrigerator. Serves 14-16.*

MIRIAM BEMAN (DEANE)
Raw Spinach Salad

1 lb. fresh spinach
6 green onions, thinly sliced
4 hard cooked eggs, coarsely
   chopped

8 crisp-cooked bacon slices,
   crumbled
dash of pepper

1 *Wash spinach. Remove stems and break leaves into bite-size pieces.*
2 *In salad bowl, lightly toss spinach with onions, eggs, bacon, and pepper.*
3 *Refrigerate, covered, about 2 hours. Serve with light salad dressing.*

TALLY MARR (DAVE)
Sensation Salad Dressing

½ lb. Romano cheese, finely
   ground
1 pt. salad oil

juice of 4 lemons
garlic powder, to taste
salt and pepper, to taste

1 *Shake all ingredients in quart jar.*
2 *Toss with lettuce and green onions.*

HELEN MURCH

Korean Salad Dressing

1 cup salad oil
½ cup vinegar
½ cup sugar
1 medium onion, chopped fine

1 tsp. Worcestershire sauce
½ tsp. salt
⅓ cup celery, chopped fine

1 *Mix vinegar, sugar, onion, Worcestershire sauce, salt, and celery in blender.*

2 *Add oil very slowly and blend again.*

3 *Toss over favorite salad ingredients and serve.*

JIMMYE AARON (TOMMY)

Congealed Salad

1 pkg. lime gelatin
1 cup boiling water
9 marshmallows, chopped
¾ cup cold water

1 small can crushed pineapple
1 pkg. cream cheese, softened
2 tbs. mayonnaise
1 cup pecans, chopped

1 *Dissolve gelatin in hot water. Add marshmallows, cold water and pineapple.*

2 *Place in refrigerator until slightly congealed.*

3 *Combine cream cheese and mayonnaise. Add to gelatin mixture. Pour in pecans and mix well. Chill and serve.*

SUZANNE MAHAFFEY (JOHN)

Spinach Salad

1 large pkg. raw spinach
1 pkg. Kraft Bleu Cheese
   crumbles

¼ cup Italian salad dressing
3-4 slices bacon, fried crisp

1 *Wash raw spinach and tear into bite-size pieces. Place in salad bowl and add Cheese Crumbles and crumbled bacon.*

2 *Toss with Italian dressing and refrigerate until chilled. Serves 6.*

ROSE ELDER (LEE)

Tuna Salad

Dressing

2 firm tomatoes, skinned
2 sweet peppers, boiled until
    soft
6-7 scallions, chopped
1 3½ oz. can tuna (packed in
    water)
2 hard boiled eggs, sliced
1 tsp. capers
2 tbs. parsley, chopped
10-15 pitted black olives

1 tbs. lemon juice
2 tbs. olive oil
Season All
black pepper
dash of sugar

1 *Slice tomatoes and peppers into narrow strips.*
2 *Combine all vegetables into large bowl.*
3 *Add tuna, drained and crumbled.*
4 *Mix dressing and pour over salad. Mix well.*

CARON RESOR (MIKE)

Caesar Salad

1 head Romaine lettuce
1 cup artichoke hearts,
    cooked and sliced
½ cup radishes, thinly sliced

½ cup swiss or jack cheese, grated
1 pkg. Caesar Salad dressing mix
½ cup saffola oil
3 tbs. fresh lemon juice

1 *Mix packaged salad dressing according to directions, but using lemon juice in place of vinegar, and saffola oil in place of salad oil.*
2 *Toss dressing with bite size pieces of lettuce, artichoke hearts, radishes, and cheese. Serve immediately.*

SUSAN NORTH (ANDY)
Salad Dressing

½ medium onion, finely
  chopped
½ oz. jar pimento, finely
  chopped
6 tbs. sugar

½ cup salad oil
1½ tsp. salt
¼ cup cider vinegar
½ green pepper, finely chopped

1 *Dissolve sugar and salt in vinegar. Add oil. Shake well.*

2 *Add chopped vegetables and mix well. Toss over favorite salad ingredients. Shake salad dressing well before each use.*

SHIRLEY LITTLER (GENE)
Garden Salad

2 carrots, grated
2 tomatoes, sliced
1 heaping tbs. mayonnaise
½ cup vinegar and oil
  dressing

1 avocado, sliced
4 heaping tbs. sunflower seeds
1 head lettuce (romaine, parsley,
  fresh spinach, or a combination)

1 *Lightly toss all ingredients in large bowl.*

2 *Add a vinegar and oil dressing of your choice.*

*"We like to use the lemons off our tree and
some apricot kernel oil and season to taste."*

KATHRYN SMITH (BOB)

(salad)
1 head iceburg lettuce
1 head red leaf lettuce
1 red onion, cut in rings
Parmesan cheese, to taste

(dressing)
1 pt. sour cream
mayonnaise, to taste
juice from 1 fresh lemon

1 *In bowl, place sour cream. Add mayonnaise, tasting until desired flavor is achieved, but leaving sour cream taste dominant. Stir in lemon juice and mix well.*

2 *Pour dressing over lettuce leaves, add Parmesan cheese and toss.*

NOTES

X

Soups

Editor's Note

SOUPS AND STEWS

*As my grandmother and mother always said,
"The best part of the soup is the broth," and
they always made their own. It was such a practical thing to do, we always had bones and
scraps of meats, etc. that were not enough for a
meal. Even the broth from fresh cooked greens
was called "pot liquor," and we all shared delicious cups of this broth. (I know my nieces and
nephews will be asking their parents, "What is
Aunt Rose talking about—what is 'pot liquor?")
Now thanks to freezers, it is so easy to accumu-
late a variety of scraps for soups and you can
make your own broth and freeze in ice cube
trays and use as needed for your various recipes. A hearty soup is often a meal itself !*

WINIFRED PALMER (ARNOLD)
Arnie's Favorite Beef Stew

2 to 3 lbs. beef, cut into
   1-inch cubes
oil
1 to 2 cups vegetable cocktail
   juice (V-8)
½ cup red table wine

1 can (10½-oz.) condensed beef
   broth
1 can (10½-oz.) mushroom gravy
fresh vegetables, cut up

1 Brown beef slowly in a small amount of oil.

2 Add vegetable juice, wine, broth and gravy. Simmer, covered, for 2 hours; then add fresh vegetables. (We like onions, carrots, potatoes and mushrooms.)

3 Cook 1 hour longer. Liquid ingredients may be increased, if necessary. Serves 6 to 8.

MARY LOU BOLT (TOMMY)
Creole Bouillabaisse

½ lb. mushrooms, sliced thinly
2 tbs. butter
2 large onions, chopped
2 cloves garlic, chopped
2 tbs. flour
2 cups tomato pulp
2 cups water
8 cloves

3 bay leaves
1½ tsp. curry powder
½ cup sherry
dash of Tabasco sauce
1 tsp. salt
4 lbs. fish fillets*
1½ qts. boiling water
hot buttered toast

*Red snapper and redfish in about equal amounts are the preferred fish for this recipe.

1 Melt butter and saute onions, garlic and flour in it until golden brown; add tomato pulp and 2 cups of water, 4 cloves, bay leaves, curry powder, ¼ cup sherry and Tabasco. Simmer for 30 minutes and season with salt.

2 Simmer fish fillets in boiling water with 4 cloves and remainder of sherry for 15 minutes. Combine mushrooms and sauce with fish and cook for 5 minutes.

3 Remove pieces of fish from sauce, place on buttered slices of toast on a large platter, pour sauce over fish and serve. Yields 12 to 15 portions.

MARY GRIER (EXCELL)

Mary's Chicken & Dumplings

1 stewing chicken (4-5 lbs.)
1 large onion
salt and pepper, to taste

2 qts. water
2½ cups flour, plain
(not self-rising)

1 *In large pot place water, chicken, onion, salt and pepper. Let come to a boil, reduce heat and simmer for ½ hour.*

2 *Remove about 3 cups of broth, set aside and cool (you may put ice cubes in to cool quickly).*

3 *Continue to simmer pot for about 2-3 hours.*

4 *For dumplings, add cooled chicken broth to flour and mix to a soft dough.*

5 *Refrigerate until chicken is done.*

6 *Roll out and cut into squares.*

7 *Remove chicken from hot stock and add dumplings while stock is still boiling. Reduce heat to low and gradually simmer for about an hour until well done.* Do Not Stir!

LABRON HARRIS, JR.

Cold Avocado Clamato Soup

3 fresh tomatoes
4 green onions
2 avocados
2 stalks celery
¼ green pepper
½ cup catsup
1 tbs. horseradish

3 tbs. Worcestershire sauce
2 tbs. lemon juice
salt and pepper
2 cans (8 oz. each) minced clams
(drain the juice from one can)
1 qt. Clamato juice

1 *Chop the tomatoes, celery, onions, green pepper and combine with the rest of the ingredients, except the avocados. Let all of this chill for at least two hours. Before serving, chop the avocados finely and add to the mixture. Serves 6.*

" . . . the more we travel, the more we treasure good food!"

ROSE ELDER (LEE)

Rose's Own Clean the Refrigerator Vegetable Stew

2 lbs. beef cubes (lean bottom round)
2½ cups water
2 tsp. marjoram
2 pkg. Spring vegetable soup
1 can condensed tomato soup
1 stick margarine
dash Tabasco
1 tbs. Accent
3 tbs. beef bouillon (or 3 cubes)
¼ cup dry red wine
6 potatoes, quartered

1 large onion, sliced
1 green pepper, diced
6 carrots, sliced
2 tomatoes, quartered
½ carton cherry tomatoes, halved
½ pkg. frozen lima beans
1 lb. 4 oz. pkg. frozen Fiesta corn
dash soy sauce
3 garlic cloves, sliced thinly
¼ pkg. frozen squash

1 *Place beef in water with marjoram, Accent, bouillon, garlic, onion, green pepper.*

2 *Cover and simmer for about 15 minutes.*

3 *Add tomato soup, vegetable soup, ½ margarine, Tabasco, soy sauce and simmer 15 minutes more.*

4 *Add potatoes, carrots, lima beans, Fiesta corn, squash and simmer 15 minutes again.*

5 *Add rest of margarine, wine and tomatoes and simmer on low flame until vegetables are tender. Do not overcook.*

ROSE ELDER (LEE)

Bull Shot Soup

1 10½ oz. can condensed beef broth, undiluted
½ soup can water
1 tbs. Worcestershire sauce

1 tsp. Season All
dash of Accent
½ cup vodka

1 *Heat broth and water just to a boil.*

2 *Stir in other ingredients; then vodka. Yields 3 servings.*

ROSE ELDER (LEE)
Chicken/Beef Soup with Oysters

1 4-lb. stewing chicken, cut up
1 lb. beef cut in cubes (try to get good beef with fat veins running through; it's very tender)
1 pkg. cut okra (about ½ lb.)
½ cup diced celery
½ cup diced onions
2½ to 3 qts. water
1 tsp. paprika
1 sprig leaf thyme
2 doz. large select oysters (preferably fresh from your seafood market)

4 good size tomatoes (or can of whole or halved tomatoes)
2 garlic cloves, diced
2 bunches chives, diced (can use frozen chives also)
1 tsp. marjoram (or more according to taste)
2 tsp. Season All
3 chicken bouillon cubes
3 tbs. margarine
1 tsp. white pepper
1 tsp. Accent

1 *Cover beef and chicken with water. Add thyme, marjoram, bouillon cubes and boil for 45 minutes or until chicken and beef are tender.*

2 *Remove and cool chicken.*

3 *Remove bone and cut into bite size cubes. Return to stock.*

4 *Add all vegetables and rest of ingredients. Cook about 30 minutes until vegetables are tender.*

5 *Add oysters; steam about 7 minutes. Serve over rice or you can add egg noodles to the soup.*

"Great with Alma Genus' cornbread!"

CLAUDIA TREVINO (LEE)
Caldillo (Mexican Stew)

2 lbs. lean beef, cubed
1 cup flour
3 tbs. vegetable oil
4 medium potatoes

1 small can chopped green chili
1 can beef stock
1 medium onion, quartered
1 can stewed tomatoes

1 *Flour and brown meat in oil.*

2 *In large sauce pan, combine other ingredients and cover with water. Simmer for 2 hours.*

3 *Salt and pepper to taste. Other spices, such as onion salt, may be added if desired.*

ROSE ELDER (LEE)

Broccoli Soup with Carrots

1 bunch fresh broccoli,
  steamed & chopped, or 2
  pkgs. frozen chopped
2 medium size carrots,
  steamed & diced
2 cans condensed cream of
  mushroom soup
8-10 fresh mushrooms, sliced
  very thin
2 cups milk

1 cup Johannesberg Reisling white
  wine
5 tbs. butter
½ tsp. tarragon, crushed
½ tsp. marjoram
¼ tsp. white pepper or to taste
1 tbs. cornstarch, mix w/milk

1 *Cook broccoli and carrots until tender in vegetable streamer. Do not over-cook. (If you don't have a steamer, use a colander over hot water.)*

2 *Place mushroom soup, milk, wine, butter, mushrooms, tarragon, marjoram, and pepper in a large pot. Add broccoli and carrots to soup. Heat thoroughly.*

3 *Yields 8 (cup) servings.*

ROSE ELDER (LEE)

Watercress Soup

1 bunch watercress
2 cans condensed consomme,
  undiluted
2 tsp. all purpose flour or
  cornstarch
4 tsp. butter or margarine,
  melted

dash of Accent
dash of Season All
1 tbs. chicken or beef broth

1 *Put watercress through meat chopper using finest blade.*

2 *Heat consomme with flavored bouillon. Add watercress.*

3 *Combine flour or cornstarch and butter; add to consomme. Serve immediately. Yields 1 quart.*

MARILYN DERMER (HAROLD)

Chicken Soup

4-5 lb. chicken
one medium onion, chopped
4 stalks celery with leaves on,
    chopped
4 quarts water

4 carrots, chopped
2 or 3 chicken bouillon cubes
    (optional)
salt and pepper to taste

1 *Place cut-up chicken in water and cook until scum forms.*
2 *Remove scum, add onion and continue cooking for one hour.*
3 *Add vegetables, salt and pepper. Cook until chicken is soft, usually about 2 hours.*
4 *Cool and remove fat that will form on top. If soup is not strong, add 2 or 3 chicken bouillon cubes. Serve with noodles or rice.*

THELMA RAUSCHER (JOE)

Tillie's Old Fashioned Barley Soup

2 lbs. short ribs of beef
4 to 5 marrow bones
1 veal bone
¼ cup carrots, diced
¼ cup celery, diced

¼ cup onions, diced
1 clove
1 bay leaf
2 tsp. salt
¾ cup pearl barley

1 *Cover meat and bones with 2½ qts. water; bring to a boil. Skim top.*
2 *Lower heat and add vegetables. Simmer 4-5 hours on low pilot light. Cool and refrigerate over night.*
3 *In the morning, remove fat and bring to a boil. Strain through cheesecloth.*
4 *Wash barley and add to 6 cups boiling water (in separate pot from soup). Cook 1 hour on low heat, stirring occasionally. Add more water if necessary. When tender, pour off excess water and add to soup. Let simmer about 30 minutes.*
5 *Remove fat from short ribs. Serve with horseradish.*

   (If additional vegetables wanted, cook separately and add to soup.)

ROSE ELDER (LEE)

Lee Elder's Quick Soup To Go With A Sandwich

1 envelope dehydrated chicken
   noodle soup mix
10 fresh mushrooms, thinly
   sliced
2 tsp. parsley, chopped
2 tbs. chives, chopped

1 beef bouillon cube
dash of Accent
dash of Season All
1 cup egg noodles
1 cup warm water

1 *Prepare soup mix according to package directions.*

2 *Add mushrooms, parsley, chives, bouillon cube and cook for about 7 minutes.*

3 *Add cup warm water and slowly add egg noodles, stirring constantly. Dash with Accent and Season All.*

4 *Cook about 5 minutes more or until noodles are done.* Do Not Overcook. *Yields 4-6 servings.*

ROSE ELDER (LEE)

Rose's Navy Bean Soup

1 lb. navy beans (baby size)
5 qts. water
2 ham hocks (smoked and
   very meaty) or left over
   chicken, beef, etc.
3 medium size potatoes, cut
   into cubes
1 cup chives, chopped
½ cup celery, chopped
3 cloves garlic, minced

1 cup carrots, diced
1 large can tomatoes
1 tbs. Season All
1 stick margarine
¼ cup parsley, chopped
3 bouillon cubes (chicken)
¼ cup fine barley (optional)
pepper, to taste

1 *Wash beans and cover with about 5 quarts of water; add ham hocks and bouillon cubes and simmer for 2½ hours or until beans are nearly tender.*

2 *Add tomatoes, celery, carrots, potatoes, chives, garlic, parsley, Season All, pepper, barley and margarine. Cook slowly for about one hour or until vegetables are tender (not overcooked).*

3 *Remove ham hocks and cut lean part into bite-size pieces. Add meat to soup beans.*

4 *Simmer, stirring occasionally to keep from sticking. You may add more water from time to time to get consistency you like. Yields about 4½ qts. I serve with hot biscuits and a tossed salad.*

GEN. DANIEL "CHAPPIE" JAMES (DOTTIE)

Okra Gumbo

2 lbs. stewing beef or veal	½ tsp. basil
2 cups water	½ tsp. oregano
2 cups onions, chopped	⅛ tsp. pepper
¾ cups green pepper, chopped	dash crushed red pepper flakes
2 cloves garlic, crushed	¼ cup flour
1½ tsp. salt	¼ cup bacon drippings
1½ tsp. gumbo file	4 fresh tomatoes, peeled &
1 tsp. sugar	quartered
¾ cup celery, chopped	1 cup tomato sauce
	1½ lbs. fresh okra, cut into ½-inch
	pieces

1 *Cut meat into 1-inch cubes.*

2 *To a heavy kettle or dutch oven, add water, onions, green pepper, celery, garlic, salt, gumbo file, sugar, basil, oregano, pepper, and red pepper flakes. (Gumbo file is innate to gumbo as far as Southern cooks are concerned, but it is not generally available in the North. It may be omitted; in which case, add a little more red pepper and herbs).*

3 *Simmer all ingredients for 1 hour. Then separate meat from broth and set both aside.*

4 *Make a brown roux with flour and bacon drippings. To the roux, add broth, tomatoes, tomato sauce and cook covered until the sauce is well blended. Then to the sauce, add the meat. Cover again and simmer gently about 45 minutes longer, stirring occasionally to prevent sticking.*

5 *Add okra to the gumbo and cook another 20-30 minutes or until okra is tender. Serve with rice. Yields 6 servings.*

SHIRLEY LITTLER (GENE)

Spinach Herb Soup

2 tsp. butter
⅓ cup green onion and tops
2 tbs. chives, finely chopped
1 cup watercress, chopped
1 tbs. parsley, finely chopped
2 cups spinach, chopped

4 cans (10 oz. size) consomme
½ tsp. salt/⅛ tsp. pepper
½ tsp. dried tarragon, crushed
½ cup light cream
1 cup lettuce, chopped

1 *Melt butter in a large sauce pan. Add green onions and tops, parsley, chives, watercress, lettuce, spinach, salt, pepper, and tarragon. Cook over low heat for 15 minutes.*

2 *Pour in consomme and continue cooking 15 minutes.*

3 *Before serving, stir in cream and bring just to a boil.*

"If you prefer a smoother textured soup, puree in blender before cooking."

JEAN WALL (ART)

Vegetable Chowder

¼ lb. bacon
4 medium onions, chopped
2 cups celery, diced
2 cups raw potatoes, diced
2 cups corn (fresh or canned)

2 cups tomatoes (fresh or canned)
1 pt. milk
2 tbs. butter
2 tbs. sugar
salt and pepper

1 *Fry bacon. Remove from skillet and saute onions in remaining bacon fat.*

2 *Return bacon to skillet. Add potatoes and celery. Cover with water. Cook slowly until tender.*

3 *Add salt, corn, tomatoes, sugar. Blend slowly ½ hour.*

4 *Add milk and butter. Heat—DO NOT BOIL. Serve immediately.*

"This can be adjusted to the family's likes and dislikes. Some cooks add leftover vegetables, such as carrots or beans. I add more bacon; use less celery. A great meal with pear or pineapple salad and hot rolls."

ROSE ELDER'S GRANDMOTHER

Nannie's Potato Soup with Dumplings

8 medium size potatoes, diced
1 can cream of mushroom
  soup
¼ pound steak of lean, sliced
  thin in strips

dash of red pepper
celery salt
parsley flakes
Janes Seasoning
1 medium size onion, diced

1 *Fry steak of lean in a heavy skillet until brown on both sides.*
2 *Cover diced potatoes well with water: add steak of lean and all drippings from skillet.*
3 *Add can of mushroom soup and rest of ingredients; allow to simmer until potatoes are tender.*
4 *Drop spoon dumplings on top and simmer for about ¾ of an hour or until dumplings are done (dumplings are done when fork comes out clean). Yields 8 servings.*

Easy Spoon Dumplings

1 *Use self rising flour and water. Mix these ingredients together to the consistency of biscuit dough. Drop small spoon fulls on top of potato soup.*

Note: My grandmother doesn't use alcoholic beverages, however, when I make this, it's excellent with a little cream sherry.—Rose.

XI

Vegetables

VEGETABLES

Vegetables are some of my favorite foods. They are truly an integral part of the preparation and style of a dish. My meals are also very colorful and attractive. I use a lot of green beans and carrots for color. I love fresh vegetables. Most of our vegetables are seasonal; and when I am not traveling, I try to freeze whatever I can for the Winter months at home. Another thing my cousin Irene taught me is to wash well the vegetables with lots of care not to bruise.

PATTI CLARKE (BUDDY)

Buddy Clarke's String Beans in Marinade

3 cans whole string beans
(canned or fresh)
1 large Spanish (or sweet)
onion, sliced
1 tsp. salt
1 tsp. pepper
1 tsp. garlic salt

1 tsp. onion salt
1 tsp. sweet basil
1 cup olive oil
½ cup wine vinegar (white or red)

1 *Drain 2 cans of beans thoroughly (use juice of one can).*

2 *Mix all ingredients, pour over stringbeans.*

3 *Set at room temperature to marinate for about 1 hour.*

4 *Put in refrigerator overnight. Serves 8-10 people.*

ROSE ELDER (LEE)

Eggplant Slices Stuffed with Cream Cheese
(A Turkish Delicacy)

2 long, large eggplants
oil
½ lb. cream cheese, Greek
Halumi or mozzarella

3-4 eggs
4 tsp. parsley, finely chopped
fine dry bread crumbs

1 *Slice the eggplants lengthwise and cut each into three to make small rectangles. Sprinkle with salt; set aside in colander for about ½ hour. (This allows bitter juices to drain and will keep them from absorbing too much oil.)*

2 *Rinse off salt with cold water and pat slices dry. Fry slices in oil just until soft and colored. Remove and drain on paper towel.*

3 *Mash cream cheese, or grate Halumi or mozzarella. Add 2 eggs, beaten and parsley. Mix well.*

4 *Spread a little of this mixture on a slice of eggplant, and layer with another slice. Continue this method of layering; the mixture will hold slices together.*

5 *Beat the remaining eggs, dip "sandwiches" in beaten egg and coat with bread crumbs.*

6 *Fry in hot oil for 2 to 3 minutes until golden. Drain on paper towels and serve hot.*

ROSE ELDER (LEE)

PETE SOPITHAKUR
Chinese Style Broccoli
(in a Wok)

1 bunch broccoli, chopped	1 tsp. soy sauce
3 tbs. peanut oil (or just	½ tsp. sugar
1 clove garlic, minced	1 tbs. corn starch
½ cup chicken broth	¼ cup water

1 *Heat wok to high temperature. Add oil and garlic. Stir. Add chopped broccoli, chicken broth, soy sauce and sugar. Stir until color changes slightly. DO NOT OVERCOOK. Mix in a cup cornstarch and water, just enough for a very thin sauce. Pour over broccoli, stir until slightly glazed.*

Pete Sopithakur has been serving Mr. and Mrs. Elder and their friends for the last 8 years at Trader Vic in Washington, D.C. He also is a regular participant in the Lee Elder Celebrity Pro-Am.

NANCY NICHOLS (BOBBY)

Baked Sweet Potatoes

(potatoes)	*(topping)*
4 medium sweet potatoes	1 cup pecans, chopped
½ cup sugar	1 cup light brown sugar
1 tsp. cinnamon	½ stick butter
½ tsp. nutmeg	
½ tsp. cloves, ground	
1 egg	
small amount of milk	
(about ¼ cup)	

1 *Preheat oven to 350°.*

2 *Boil potatoes until tender; remove peelings and mash together in a bowl with other ingredients.*

3 *Put into glass baking dish (1½ to 2-qt. size). Set aside.*

4 *For topping, mix the ingredients and spread over top of mashed potato mixture. Bake in covered dish for 45 minutes to 1 hour.*

"A recipe that Bobby really enjoys. It's a dish that is particularly good for the Holidays. We always have it for Thanksgiving and Christmas."

JOAN NIEPORTE (TOM)

Baked Stuffed Cabbage

2 large heads cabbage
2 lbs. chuck, ground
1 lb. lean pork, ground
1 cup Minute rice
1 large onion, grated
4 eggs
4-8-oz. cans tomatoes

salt and pepper, to taste
4-8-oz. cans stewed tomatoes or
   soup
juice of 1 lemon
1 tsp. sugar

1 Boil cabbage for 5 minutes, or until leaves are soft and easy to roll.
2 Heat oven to 350°.
3 Combine meat, rice, onion, eggs, salt and pepper. Mix well and form into mound of meat.
4 Place mount of meat mixture on cabbage leaf and fold over.
5 Place in roasting pan, cover and bake for one hour.
6 Mix tomatoes, soup, salt, lemon juice, and sugar. After meat loaf has baked for 1 hour, pour sauce over and bake 45 minutes longer.

SIS GOEKEN (RICHARD)

Marinated Cauliflower

1 head cauliflower, cut into
   flowerettes
3 carrots, peeled, cut into
   2-inch strips
1 green pepper, cut into 2-inch
   strips
¾ cup white vinegar
2 tbs. sugar

½ tsp. oregano
4 stalks celery, cut into ½-inch
   pieces
1 jar small stuffed olives, cut in
   half
½ cup oil
1 tsp. salt
¼ cup water

1 Combine all ingredients in large pot. Cover and bring to boil.
2 Reduce heat, simmer for 5 minutes only.
3 Cool, then refrigerate 24 hours. Serve on chopped lettuce.

CAROLYN DICKSON (BOB)

Green Enchiladas

1 doz. corn tortillas	¼ cup oleo margarine
½ cup cooking oil	¼ cup flour
8 oz. Monterey Jack cheese, shredded	2 cups chicken broth
	1 cup sour cream
¾ cup onion, chopped	1 4-oz. can diced green chillies

1 In skillet, cook tortillas one at a time in hot oil until soft. (Don't overcook or they won't roll.)

2 Put 2 tbs. of cheese and one tbs. of onion on each tortilla and roll. Put in oblong casserole dish.

3 In saucepan, blend flour and oleo, add broth and cook until it thickens and bubbles. Stir in sour cream and chopped peppers. Blend well, but do not boil or it will curdle.

4 Pour over rolled tortillas and bake at 425° about 20 minutes.

MIRIAM BEMAN (DEANE)

Crab-Stuffed Potatoes

4 medium Idaho potatoes	1 tsp. salt
1 6-oz. can crabmeat	¼ tsp. onion, grated
½ cup butter	1 cup sharp cheese, grated
½ cup light cream	½ tsp. paprika
	¼ tsp. cayenne

1 Scrub potatoes well and bake in slow oven until you can pierce easily with fork.

2 When cooled, cut potatoes in half, lengthwise and scoop out potato.

3 Using mixer, whip potatoes with butter, cream, salt, paprika, onion and cheese.

4 Drain crabmeat and with a fork or spoon, mix in crabmeat and refill the potato shells. Sprinkle with paprika and reheat in low oven about 15 minutes.

"May be made in advance, frozen, and reheated in hot oven for about a half hour before serving. Delicious accompaniment with broiled steaks and a salad."

DONNA ARCHER (GEORGE)

Vegetable Medley

2 boxes frozen broccoli
1 jar marinated artichoke
   hearts
3 cups white sauce
¾ cup cheddar cheese, grated

½ cup mayonnaise
1 tbs. horseradish
salt and pepper, to taste
1 can bamboo shoots
1 4-oz. can sliced mushrooms

1 *Cook broccoli according to directions.*

2 *Add cheese to heated white sauce. Stir until melted, remove from heat. Add mayonnaise, horseradish, salt and pepper.*

3 *In a 2½ to 3-qt. casserole dish alternate layers of all vegetables and pour sauce over; top with additional melted cheese.*

4 *Bake in 350 to 375° oven for 30 to 45 minutes. Yields 8 servings.*

MARY HARRIS (LABRON)

Stuffed Tomatoes

6 tomatoes
3 stalks celery
3 sprigs parsley
2 small carrots
1 large onion
1½ cup raw spinach

1 small green pepper
3 tbs. butter, melted
¾ cup bread crumbs
⅓ cup milk
1 egg, beaten
Parmesan cheese

1 *Cut thin slice from the tops of tomatoes and scoop out the seeds and pulp. Salt these shells and invert to drain for 15 minutes.*

2 *Chop the celery, parsley, carrots, spinach, onion and pepper very fine. Then saute these vegetables in butter until the onion is golden brown.*

3 *Stir in the bread crumbs, milk and egg. Salt and pepper to taste.*

4 *Combine all the ingredients, pack into the tomato shells and sprinkle generously with grated parmesan cheese. Place in a buttered baking dish and bake at 400° for 20 minutes. Yields 6 servings.*

BRENDA DENT (JIM)

Cabbage with Okra

1 white or green cabbage
1 lb. medium to small okra,
   with ends snipped
2 strips bacon or salt pork

½ cup water
½ tsp. salt

1 *Fry bacon until crisp. Remove from skillet and drain off all fat except 1 tbs.*
2 *Add water and salt to remaining fat. Cover and simmer while you separate cabbage leaves.*
3 *Place cabbage leaves in skillet and simmer for 5 minutes.*
4 *Place okra on top of cabbage and simmer over low heat until tender.*
5 *Just before serving, crumble bacon strips and sprinkle over vegetables.*

ROSE ELDER (LEE)

Marinated Vegetables

1 bunch broccoli, cut up
1 head cauliflower, cut in
   flowerettes
1 bunch medium size carrots,
   cut in half and sliced

1 lb. fresh mushrooms, sliced
Accent
Season All

1 *Steam all vegetables separately until tender but still crunchy (don't overcook).*
2 *Sprinkle with Accent and Season All.*
3 *Pour marinade over steamed vegetables—serve hot or cold.*

Marinade

2 garlic cloves, minced
¾ cup white wine vinegar
1 16-oz bottle Wish Bone
   Italian Dressing

¾ cup red or white wine
   (optional)
1 tsp. oregano

"A great buffet dish!
Better the next day after refrigerated."

ROSE ELDER (LEE)

Eggplant Parmagiana

⅓ cup milk
2 eggs
1 tsp. Italian seasoning
cooking oil
1 large eggplant, cut in ¼-inch
    slices

1 can Ragu cooking sauce (16 oz.)
½ cup sharp cheese, shredded
8 oz. mozzarella cheese, shredded
¼ cup medium dry red wine

1 *In mixing bowl, combine milk, eggs and Italian seasoning.*

2 *Dip eggplant in mixture and coat well.*

3 *In a large skillet over low heat, put 2 tbs. oil and fry eggplant until golden brown on both sides, cooking a few pieces at a time. Add more oil as needed.*

4 *Remove eggplant, drain on paper towel.*

5 *Oil a 12-inch baking dish. Layer with eggplant slices, layer of tomato sauce, mixed with wine, then layer of cheese. Repeat all steps until all ingredients are used.*

6 *Bake at 350° in preheated oven for 20 minutes or until bubbly. Serves 6.*

JOANNE KOHLER (ROY)

Tomato Mince Meat

12 green tomatoes, grind
6 pears, grind
9 large apples, grind
4½ cups seedless raisins
3 oranges, coarsely ground
3 tbs. lemon rind, grated
1 cup cider vinegar
⅓ cup orange juice

⅓ cup lemon juice
3 cups molasses
1 cup brown sugar
2 tbs. cinnamon
1½ tsp. nutmeg
1½ tsp. ginger
1½ tsp. allspice
1½ tsp. ground cloves
1½ tsp. salt

1 *Place all ingredients except spices in a kettle and boil about 30 minutes until it thickens; then add spices.*

2 *Cook 5 minutes more and put in jars. Four cups makes one pie. Or you may use the water bath and boil 20 minutes, seal and put away.*

JUDY ERSKINE (RANDY)

Cheese and Potato Casserole

2 lb. pkg. frozen hash browns
2 cans cheddar cheese soup
(10 oz. cans)
1 can evaporated milk,
undiluted (13 oz. can)

1 can french fried onion rings
salt and pepper, to taste

1 Combine frozen vegetables, soup, milk and half the onion rings in a greased Crockpot.
2 Add salt and pepper then cover and cook on low 8-9 hours or on high 4 hours.
3 Sprinkle remaining onion rings over top before serving.

"This recipe could also be used without a crockpot. Cooking time in a regular pot on the stove top is 40-60 minutes."

GAIL MURPHY (BOB)

Cheddar Squash Bake

2 lbs. zucchini squash
2 egg yolks, slightly beaten
1 cup sour cream
2 tbs. all-purpose flour

2 egg whites, beaten until stiff
1½ cups cheddar cheese,
shredded
6 slices bacon, fried and
crumbled
2 tbs. butter, melted

1 Wash squash, trim ends, and boil in salted water for 15 minutes.
2 Drain squash thoroughly and slice, reserving a few slices for garnish.
3 Mix together egg yolks, sour cream and flour. Fold in egg whites.
4 Layer half the squash, egg mixture and cheese in 2-qt. baking dish. Sprinkle with bacon. Repeat layers until dish is filled.
5 Mix bread crumbs and butter together and smooth on top of casserole. Arrange reserved squash on top. Bake in 350° oven for 20-25 minutes.

PATRICIA SPAULDING (AARON)

Fried Cabbage

1 head cabbage, coarsely
  shredded
1 medium onion, quartered

3 strips bacon
salt and pepper, to taste

1 *In heavy iron skillet, fry bacon until crisp. Remove and set aside.*

2 *Pour off bacon fat, except about 2 tbs., and to same skillet, add cabbage and onion, seasoning with salt and pepper. (I prefer a peppery taste so I season generously with pepper). Fry cabbage and onions in skillet over medium heat until vegetables are transparent.* Do not add water *as vegetables make their own juice. Also,* do not overcook. *Vegetables should be slightly crisp when served.*

3 *Sprinkle with crumbled bacon and serve immediately. Serves 6.*

SHIRLEY LITTLER (GENE)

Mock Broccoli Souffle

3 tbs. flour
3 tbs. butter, melted
½ cup milk

4 eggs, beaten until light
1 tbs. onion juice
½ cup mayonnaise
1½ pkg. frozen broccoli

1 *Mix flour, butter and milk until smooth in bowl.*

2 *In separate dish, combine eggs with onion juice, mayonnaise and broccoli.*

3 *Thoroughly mix egg and broccoli mixture with white sauce.*

4 *Place in buttered 1½-qt. baking dish and bake at 350° for 45 minutes.*

JEAN PAYNE (REUBEN)

Cabbage Suisada

1 cup cabbage, shredded
1 clove garlic, minced
1 oz. onion, sliced

¼ cup water
¼ medium tomato, diced
4 oz. cooked shrimp

1 *In non-stick skillet, combine cabbage, garlic, onion and water. Cook over low heat 4 minutes or until cabbage is just tender.*

2 *Add tomato and shrimp; cook an additional 2 minutes or until heated throughout. Yields one serving.*

SCOTTY SANDERS (DOUG)

Turnip Greens

**3 lbs. fresh turnip greens   ½ lb. salt pork or ham hocks
   with turnip bulks**

1 *Wash greens several times. Peel and slice turnip bulbs and set aside.*

2 *Boil meat covered with water in a large pot for 20 minutes.*

3 *Add greens and bring to a boil. Cover and lower heat—cook slowly for 2 hours.*

4 *Add peeled and slices turnip bulbs on top of greens and cook for 20 minutes more.*

JILL McGEE (JERRY)

Sliced Baked Potatoes

1 *Slice raw potatoes very thin.*

2 *Heavily baste with butter, salt and pepper. Put into casserole dish in preheated oven at 350°, cook for 20 minutes, turning on both sides, or until tender.*

BETTY ALTOMONTE (JOE)

Fried Cauliflower

**1 head cauliflower   scant ¼ cup parmesan cheese
flour   salt
3 eggs, beaten   cooking oil**

1 *Break cauliflower into pieces and cook in salted water until fork tender. Do not overcook.*

2 *Drain off water. Cool completely.*

3 *Dredge pieces with flour.*

4 *Add cheese to beaten eggs. Coat cauliflower with egg mixture.*

5 *Fry in 2 to 3 inches of oil until golden.*

6 *Remove pieces, drain off oil. Sprinkle on more cheese if desired. Good for a side dish or canape. Yields 6 servings.*

"Men adore this."

BETTY ALTOMONTE (JOE)

Celery Almondine

2 tbs. butter
⅓ cup almonds (blanched whole)
4 cups diagonally sliced celery
1 cube chicken bouillon, crumbled

1 tbs. instant onion, minced
1 tsp. Accent
½ tsp. sugar (white)
⅛ tsp. ginger powder

1 *Melt butter on low heat. Add almonds. Brown lightly.*

2 *Stir in remainder of ingredients.*

3 *Toss. Heat through, approximately 8 to 10 minutes. Celery remains crunchy. Yields 4-6 servings.*

LYNN GIEBERGER (ALLEN)

Scalloped Potatoes and Carrots

3 tbs. butter
6-7 carrots, peeled and sliced ⅛-inch thick
4-5 long white California potatoes, peeled and sliced ⅛-inch thick

salt
several twists of white pepper mill
2 cups heavy cream
6-7 green onion bulbs, minced

1 *Combine 2 tbs. of the butter, the carrots, onions, a good pinch of salt and about 1 cup of water in a heavy sauce pan.*

2 *Bring to a boil, reduce heat to simmer and cook 20-30 minutes or until the carrots are tender and all liquid has evaporated.*

3 *Take the remaining butter and rub onto bottom and sides of a two-quart baking dish that can go to the table. Starting with the potatoes, make layers of potatoes and carrots, finishing with potatoes. Sprinkle each layer with salt and freshly ground pepper.*

4 *Add the cream to the dish.*

5 *Place in a preheated 325° oven and bake for about one hour until potatoes are tender when pierced with a sharp knife; top should be lightly brown. Yields 6 servings.*

ROSE ELDER (LEE)

Bean Fritters

1 cup ½-inch pieces fresh
  green beans
1 cup ½-inch pieces fresh wax
  beans
1 tsp. Accent
¼ cup very thick sliced onion
1½ cups all-purpose flour

3 tsp. baking powder
¾ tsp. Season All
1 beaten egg
1 cup milk

1 *Cook green beans, wax beans and onions covered in small amount of boiling water until tender (about 30 minutes) or if using canned beans, heat onions in juice from the canned beans first with Accent, then add beans and heat thoroughly.*

2 *Stir together flour, baking powder, Season All.*

3 *Combine egg, milk, beans, and onions and add to dry ingredients.*

4 *Mix just until moistened and drop batter by tablespoons into deep hot oil. Fry until golden brown about 3 or 4 minutes.*

5 *Drain on paper towel. Yield: About 24 vegetable fritters.*

SCOTTY SANDERS (DOUG)

Baked Squash

4 to 6 medium size acorn
  squash, washed and cut in
  half
4 slices bacon, baked and
  crumbled

salt and pepper to taste
brown sugar

1 *Preheat oven to 350°.*

2 *Place bacon in shallow baking dish, bake until crisp. Remove and drain on paper towel. Cool and crumble—set aside.*

3 *Place cut side of squash down in baking dish with bacon drippings.*

4 *Bake about 1 hour or until squash is tender.*

5 *Remove and top with crumbled bacon and sprinkle lightly with brown sugar. Yields 4 servings.*

CAROL REASOR (MIKE)

Twice Baked Potatoes

4 large baking potatoes
½ cup butter
½ cup milk

½ cup grated cheese (mild or
salt and pepper to taste
paprika

1 *Preheat oven to 400° and bake potatoes for 1 hour or until soft.*

2 *Cut potatoes lengthwise, and carefully scoop out insides into mixing bowl.*

3 *Add milk, butter, salt, pepper and mix well with a beater; place back into potato jackets.*

4 *Sprinkle tops with grated cheese and paprika.*

5 *Place into 350° oven for 15 to 20 minutes before serving. Yields 8 servings.*

   NOTE: This can be prepared in the morning and placed into the oven with topping just before serving.

ROSE ELDER (LEE)

Sweet Potatoes in Amaretto Sauce

3 lbs. sweet potatoes
1 cup firmly packed brown
   sugar
½ tbs. cornstarch
⅛ tsp. ground cinnamon

⅛ cup Amaretto (Italian
   liqueur)
½ cup hot water
2 tbs. orange rind, grated
4 tbs. butter or margarine

1 *Boil sweet potatoes covered in water until tender. Drain and cool.*

2 Peel potatoes and cut in half lengthwise. Place in a 2-qt. shallow casserole dish.

3 *Combine sugar, cornstarch, cinnamon and nutmeg in a saucepan. Add Amaretto, water, and orange rind. Bring to a full boil, stirring constantly.*

4 *Remove from heat. Stir in butter (if desired).*

5 *Pour sauce over potatoes so that all are glazed and bake, uncovered at 350° for 25 minutes or until sauce is bubbly. Yields 6 to 8 servings.*

SHARON WINTZ (GARY)

Easy Eggplant Parmesan

2 large eggplants, peeled and
   cut into ½-inch thick slices
1½ cup dried bread crumbs
2 eggs, beaten
2 tbs. water

1½ cup grated Parmesan cheese
1 pkg. mozzarella cheese,
   shredded (8 oz.)
1 jar Ragu spaghetti sauce with
   meat (15½ oz. jar)
oil for frying

1 In a bowl, combine eggs and water. Dip slices of eggplant first into egg mixture and then into bread crumbs.

2 Fry eggplant slices in hot oil until brown and crisp on both sides. Drain on paper towels.

3 Layer alternately in a baking dish, sauce, eggplant, mozzarella cheese and Parmesan cheese until all ingredients are used. Bake at 325° for 45 minutes until bubbly. Yields 4 servings.

ROSE ELDER (LEE)

Broccoli and Ham Roll-up

1 bunch fresh broccoli or 1
   pgk. frozen broccoli spears,
   cooked and drained
5 thin slices of cooked ham
½ cup mayonnaise
3 tbs. flour

½ tsp. season salt
⅛ tsp. seasoned pepper
1½ cups milk
⅓ cup cheddar cheese, grated
fine dry bread crumbs

1 Roll ham around broccoli spears. Place rolls in shallow casserole dish.

2 In a small saucepan, stir together mayonnaise, flour, salt and pepper. Gradually stir in milk. Cook over low heat, stirring constantly until thickened.

3 Add cheese, stirring until blended. Pour sauce over rolls. Sprinkle with bread crumbs.

4 Broil close to source of heat for about 2 minutes or until it's bubbly. Serves about 4 or 5.

LYNN GEIBERGER (ALLEN)

Scalloped Potatoes

1 bunch carrots, very thinly
   sliced
4 to 6 white potatoes, very thinly
   sliced
6 to 8 scallions, very thinly
   sliced

1½ cups heavy cream
salt and pepper to taste
½ stick butter

1 *Layer carrots, potatoes, butter and scallions alternately in baking casserole.*

2 *Salt and pepper to taste, and pour cream over the mixture.*

3 *Bake in preheated oven at 375° for 40 minutes or until fork tender. Yields 4 servings.*

LINDA LESLIE (PERRY)

Hot Cabbage Head

1 head cabbage or chinese
   cabbage
2 tbs. dry mustard
½ tsp. salt

2 tbs. soy sauce
2 tsp. vinegar

1 *Discard any tough outer cabbage leaves. Cut cabbage into 1-inch slices across the head and boil for about 4-5 minutes. Do not overcook. Drain.*

2 *Mix remaining ingredients together in a large bowl. Add cabbage, toss to mix, cover and cool. Good at room temperature. This is very hot!*

NANCY HEARD (JERRY)

Artichokes

4 large artichokes
2 tbs. apple cider vinegar

melted butter or mayonnaise

1 *Shower artichokes with cold running water and soak 5 minutes.*

2 *Cut stems off even with base and pull off small outer leaves around the bottom.*

3 *Put into salted boiling water with vinegar. Simmer 45 minutes or until tender. Serve with melted butter or mayonnaise.*

BECKIE WIECHERS

(Jim Wiechers' mother)

Corn Tamale Dish

1 or 2 (17 oz.) cans of cream corn
1 or 2 (12 oz.) cans of whole kernel corn
½ or 1 (17 oz.) can of tamales
American cheese

1 Break tamales up into small pieces and mix with corn in a casserole dish.

2 Add the juice from the tamales and mix.

3 Sprinkle American cheese on top and heat in 350° oven, for about 30 minutes until bubbling.

"Very good with barbecued spare-ribs."

ROSE ELDER (LEE)

(From Alma Genus)

Alma's Cabbage and Okra

1 medium size head cabbage, sliced
2 stalks celery, diced
1 green pepper, diced
1 large onion, diced
bacon bits with bacon fat, 4 slices
1 large pkg. frozen okra
1 large or 2 medium tomatoes, peeled and diced

1 Cook bacon until crisp. Remove and leave fat drippings in pan.

2 Add cabbage and steam about 15 minutes.

3 Add celery, green pepper, onion and okra. Steam until tender. Do not over-cook.

4 Add tomatoes and fold in bacon bits. Yields 6 servings.

ROSE ELDER (LEE)

Lee's Favorite Sweet Potatoes

3 lbs. sweet potatoes
1 stick margarine or butter
1 cup sugar

juice of half a fresh lemon
⅛ tsp. nutmeg
⅛ tsp. Accent (dash)

1 Boil sweet potatoes in water with dash of Accent until tender. Drain and cool.

2 Peel potatoes and cut in half lengthwise.

3 Place in a 2-qt. shallow casserole dish.

4 Sprinkle with lemon juice, cinnamon, nutmeg. Cut butter or margarine into pats and place on top of potatoes. Pour sugar over top.

5 Bake, uncovered, in oven at 350° for 30 minutes or until all sugar and butter has been absorbed. Do not overcook. Serve hot. Yields about 6 servings.

SHERYL LOTT (LYN)

Broccoli Casserole

2 pkgs. broccoli, chopped
1 cup mayonnaise
1 can mushroom soup

1 cup sharp cheddar cheese,
1 cup Cheese Ritz crackers,
   crumbled
2 eggs, beaten

1 Mix broccoli, soup, cheese, and mayonnaise in bowl. Add eggs and mix well.

2 Place in buttered casserole dish. Top with cracker crumbs and bake at 350° for 35 to 40 minutes.

NOTES

Index

The Golfer's Cookbook

A personal fund raising project of Rose Elder for the benefit of the Lee Elder Scholarship Foundation.

I hope you will order additional books for your friends. For each additional cookbook, please send $8.95 plus $1.50 for postage and handling. ($2.00 for Canada and other countries.)

Make checks payable to:
The Golfer's Cookbook
and send to:
Golfer's Cookbook
1701 Taylor Street, N.W.
Washington, D.C. 20011

For special gift orders, please include instructions.